Heaven
Heals

Finding Hope in the Reunion
with Your Lost Loved One

KRISTIN LANDGREN

Praise for Heaven Heals

"*Heaven Heals* is a well-written Bible-based book that will bring readers a God-sized transformation! Kristy does a magnificent job of showing how she used the power of hope, faith and love to climb out of the valley and rise up to a victorious mountaintop."

—Dr. David Friedman Syndicated TV and Radio Health Expert, International-award winning; #1 best-selling author of *Food Sanity;* DoctorDavidFriedman.com

"Kristy Landgren's book, *Heaven Heals,* is a wonderful testament of God's love for all His children. Kristy lost her brother to mental illness at an early age, yet she overcame grief and found meaning and hope through God's eternal covenant. She explains scriptural stories in plain and simple language, providing clarity of mind and a closeness to God deeper than the layperson might have ever experienced. All the while, she shows us how she gained hope from God's promises of old and how these promises are still alive and thriving today for everyone to enjoy. For anyone who has experienced the loss of a loved one or grief of any kind and who might question God's love, this book will bring comfort and peace to the soul."

—Nanette O'Neal, author of the fantasy series *A Doorway Back to Forever*; NanetteONeal.com

Heaven Heals

Finding Hope in the Reunion with Your Lost Loved One

Kristin Landgren

Landgren Publishing

P.O. Box 24865
Los Angeles, CA 90024

Library of Congress Catalogue Number: 2020921243

Softcover: 978-0-578-76081-0
Hardcover: 978-0-578-76082-7
E-book: 978-0-578-76083-4

All Bible text throughout the book is taken from the New Living Translation and the King James Version (KJV).

Scripture quotations marked (NLT) are taken from the Holy Bible, New Living Translation, copyright ©1996, 2004, 2015 by Tyndale House Foundation. Used by permission of Tyndale House Publishers, Inc., Carol Stream, Illinois 60188. All rights reserved.

Because of the dynamic nature of the Internet, any web addresses or links may have been changed since publication and may no longer be valid.

Any people depicted in stock imagery by Getty Images are models, and such images are being used for illustrative purposes only. Certain stock imagery © Getty Images.

First Printing: 2021

Los Angeles Temple photograph: Todd Johnson Photography

Author photograph: Mark and Shelly Photography

Kristin Landgren

Landgren Publishing

P.O. Box 24865
Los Angeles, CA 90024

Interior Image Credit: Getty Images, Kristin Landgren

For previous *Heaven Heals* Companion Music CD and other works,
please visit https://www.kristylandgren.com

DEDICATION

To all who gravitate towards light,

search for truth,

sing of life,

treasure nature's beauty,

seek clarity,

love unconditionally,

and thank heaven above

CONTENTS

PREFACE

As every reader knows, adversity, even the daily struggle, can sometimes make for difficult times. Ideally, everyone has experienced warm and fulfilling relationships that make the journey a discovery of joy. Even though life bruises the spirit along the way, who hasn't stared eagerly at the stars, hoping for inspiration to questions or concerns, or gazed boldly across the ocean's grandeur, yearning for excitement and adventure, or courageously imagined what majesty lies beyond the horizon and wondered if dreams are truly achievable? What if heaven is closer than imagined or more accessible than believed? And what if pain and sadness can be soothed with the reality of love and power that is absolute, even palpable? It is with these thoughts and emotions I present this material with the intent that hope breeds faith, perspective increases knowledge, experience achieves greatness, and relationships propel eternity.

Our birth is but a sleep and a forgetting:

The Soul that rises with us, our life's Star

Hath had elsewhere its setting

And cometh from afar:

Not in entire forgetfulness

And not in utter nakedness

HEAVEN HEALS

But trailing clouds of glory do we come

From God, who is our home:

Heaven lies about us in our infancy!

(lines 58–66)

William Wordsworth; 1804, *Ode: Intimations of Immortality
from Recollections of Early Childhood*

1
THE BIBLE

I t was the best of times; it was the worst of times[1]—a lot like today. Okay, okay, Charles Dickens' renowned words were used in relating a tale of two European cities during the French Revolution. But those words seem as applicable today in their description of a modern tale of evil, one that seems to be intensifying against that which has always been recognized as good. In the 21st century, bountiful evidence of "the best of times" is observed in the proliferation of technological developments, medical advancements, and in the worldwide accessibility of information. In contrast, indications of "the worst of times" are manifest in the deteriorating biblical-based society, which reflects a decrease in personal accountability, spirituality, and in respect for others and for authority. Along with personal decline comes an increased entitlement culture and an ever-growing incivility. Diminished integrity then leads to subsequent misbehavior and crime. Adding to social unrest is a global war on terror, which aligns a radicalized Middle Eastern philosophy against Western civilization. How could we have come to this? Such a world-view clash is based on a completely misunderstood biblical teaching known as *Abraham's Covenant,* or *The Abrahamic Covenant.* Understanding this biblical doctrine allows an insight into the East/West clash and into the deterioration of modern society, a deterioration which fulfills those prophetic words in Isaiah 5:20 (KJV), referencing those ". . . that call evil good and good evil."

1

In this present climate of crumbling culture, how *does* an understanding of Abraham's Covenant enlighten the perspective and allow heaven to heal the heavy heart? Well, there is a story that goes along with this book—my story. It is the reason the book was written. I found hope in the reunion with my lost loved one, and maybe my tale will assist heaven in igniting that same spark of hope for you. Although I traveled a long road of recovery in my personal healing, an insight into the meaning of this covenant will reveal a shortcut along the path to your recovery. So, let's start, "in the beginning," with Sarah and Abraham's ancient love story, as told in the established societal centerpiece: The Bible.

The book of Genesis tells that the prophet, Abraham, was originally named Abram, and his wife, Sarah, was originally called Sarai. Abram was from Ur of the Chaldees but, following his brother's death, his family left their home in Ur. Abram's father, Terah, and his nephew, Lot, all migrated with him and Sarai to Haran, where they settled.

In Genesis chapter twelve, we first learn of God's covenant with Abram, his divine call, and God's instructions that he flee Haran and go to the land of Canaan. "The Lord had said to Abram, "Leave your native country, your relatives, and your father's family and go to the land that I will show you" Gen. 12:1 (NLT). In this same verse of The King James Version of the Bible, it implies that God warned Abram to leave the land of Haran because of danger from unrighteousness. The backdrops in Genesis 11 and 13 were depictions of the people's vain imaginations of reaching heaven by building the Tower of Babel and the wickedness of Sodom and Gomorrah. "Now the Lord said unto Abram, Get thee out of thy country, and from thy kindred, and from thy father's house, unto a land that I will show thee" Gen. 12:1 (KJV). God then declared his calling and blessing of Abram (who would come to be known throughout the ages as *Father Abraham*). "And I will make of thee a great nation, and I will bless thee, and make thy name great, and thou shalt be a blessing; and I will bless them that bless thee and curse him that curseth thee; and in thee shall all the families of the earth be blessed" Gen. 12:2-3 (KJV).

"So, Abram departed as the Lord had instructed, and Lot went with him. Abram was seventy-five years old when he left Haran. He took his wife, Sarai, his nephew Lot, and all his wealth—his livestock and all the people he had taken into his household at Haran—and headed for the land of Canaan. When they arrived in Canaan, Abram traveled through the land as far as Shechem. There he set up camp beside the oak of Moreh. At that time, the area was inhabited by Canaanites" Gen.12:4-6 (NLT). "And the Lord appeared unto Abram and said, "Unto thy seed will I give this land. And there built he an altar to the Lord. . ." Gen.12:7 (KJV).

After building the altar to give thanks to God and to pray for the people in Canaan, Abram continued his journey, sojourning southward to Egypt because of a severe famine in the land. Now, since his wife was beautiful and he was a wealthy man with many flocks, herds, gold and silver, he began to fear that he would be killed and she would be taken by the princes to Pharaoh. In these precarious circumstances, it was custom during these times for the men to devise a plan—she would claim to be his sister. This was done to save his life and property. Upon arrival in Egypt, indeed, they were separated. Even though he was treated well by the Egyptians (because they thought he was her brother), they stole Sarai away to Pharaoh's palace. Consequently, the Lord sent plagues to afflict Pharaoh's household, attempting to disrupt his designs to marry her. When Pharaoh discovered Abram and Sarai were a married couple, he was angry and sent them out of Egypt, and they returned to Canaan. "Why saidst thou: she is my sister? ...I might have taken her to me to wife. Now, therefore behold thy wife, and take her, and go thy way. And Pharaoh commanded his men . . . and they sent him away, and his wife, and all that he had"[2] Gen. 12:19-20 (KJV).

Abram and Sarai were devoted to each other and, like other dedicated couples, they were searching for a chance at a happy life of faith and family. God had promised Abram an everlasting seed, or posterity, which would become a great nation, blessing the entire earth. Because of Abram's great faith, he believed God. But both

Sarai and Abram were getting old and he wondered how he would even have a child, since Sarai was barren. God reiterated He would create a covenant with Abram but, thus far, the means by which this covenant would be established had remained vague. So, as was customary of the times, Sarai gave her handmaiden, Hagar, to Abram, possibly thinking she might provide children. Hagar gave birth to Ishmael. Then an angel pronounced to Hagar that although Ishmael's posterity would be greatly increased, Ishmael would be a wild man who would fight against every man and every man against him. Nevertheless, he would dwell among his brotherhood of men.[3] Evidently, and according to the angel, Ishmael did not seem to be the child who would establish the covenant, fulfilling the promise, ". . . in thee shall all the families of the earth be blessed."

Finally, in Genesis 17, when Abram and Sarai were both very old, God revealed the terms of his covenant to Abram. He changed his name to Abraham as a symbol of the renewal that would result from his covenant to recommit to God. God also told him Sarai

would have her name changed to Sarah, symbolic of her spiritual renewal and inclusion within the covenant. At long last, they would finally have a son. His name would be Isaac with whom the covenant would be established, and Sarah would give birth to him within the next year. (Detailed terms of their covenant with God are discussed in Chapter 3.)

The Bible stories and messages of hope and faith, such as Sarah and Abraham's, were considered indispensable by many of the early biblical scholars and reformers. They worked courageously to facilitate societies that could blossom when built upon a biblical foundation. William Tyndale is credited with the translation of the Hebrew and Greek Bibles into English—The King James Version. David Rosen, a rabbi of the Chief Rabbinate of Israel, speaking of the film, "Fires of Faith: The Coming Forth of the King James Bible,"[4] said in the film there is nothing that compares to the classical English literary resource as the King James Bible. "The closest things, of course, are the works of Shakespeare, and we do relish and treasure Shakespeare," he said. "But it doesn't speak to our deepest commitments, obviously, as the Bible does."[5] Phrases such as, *"Let there be light, Seek and ye shall find,* and *Consider the lilies of the field, how they grow,"* are among those universally recognized expressions of Tyndale's artistry as he translated the Holy Bible into English.

Many adaptations of Tyndale's Bible were to come. Two such modifications were The Living Bible, followed by The New Living Translation. These Bibles were adapted with the intention of making Scripture more easily understood in modern English. A part of the reason behind adapting the language for accessibility was the premise that more people would hear the Bible read aloud in a church service than were likely to read it or study it on their own.[6] Even though there was value in making the translation easier to understand, it is considered less accurate than the literal method of translation, which was used by Tyndale in his undertaking of the translation of the King James Version. For this reason, both The King James and New Living Translation versions are applied appropriately throughout this book.

Tyndale was influenced by John Wycliffe and by contemporary reformers of the 16th century, such as Martin Luther and John Rogers. He wanted the common man to have the Scriptures in his native tongue. At that time, only the clergy was allowed access to them. In 1408, a decree known as the Constitutions of Oxford made it illegal to translate the Bible into English, punishable by imprisonment, torture, or death.[7] Still, Tyndale worked tirelessly at his own great peril; he persevered in his translation of the English Bible, which he believed should be in every home. He is among the most revered and beloved biblical scholars of all time. Eventually, he was betrayed, charged with heresy, and died a martyr's death by hanging and burning at the stake for spreading biblical truths among his fellow citizens.

Although Tyndale is honored for his contribution of the English Bible to the church, scholars agree some translation errors do exist. In addition, "there were likely some errors that had crept in, or 'read into' the verses, due to personal biases, prejudices, or long-held church doctrines of that time."[8] Some principles or doctrines may have been omitted due to misunderstanding or judging them to be confusing or irrelevant.

* * *

My tale began in a Swedish-American community—a town of conservative, hard-working, reserved old Swedes. My grandparents taught my father a love of the Bible and, he passed that same love on to me. Faith and family were the priority. I was the oldest to my three younger siblings (one more was to come later). We had four cousins who lived in the house behind ours. When we outgrew the houses, we moved two blocks west and they moved on the same street as we did, one block south. Four of us, four of them, and we frolicked cheerfully (with the occasional spat) throughout the neighborhood, at church, after school, and in local activities. The brother closest in age to me was especially amusing and we hung around with our two cousins of similar ages. We were companions, pals, and imaginative adventurers.

But my brother was a star-studded showman. Even at my earliest memories, he was a most charming and adorable character. He was a friendly, social child with the same amazingly theatrical talents as our mother. Although I inherited her musical knack, he inherited the whole package: musical, conversational, comedic, spontaneous, entertaining, and a crowd-pleasing favorite with the singing voice of an angel. As a youngster, I thought my life was idyllic. Looking back, it seemed as picturesque as a Normal Rockwell classic. But one spring day, that was all about to change.

It was a typical occurrence for us to shuttle back and forth between houses, one block apart. This day was no exception. After school, my brother had been summoned up the street and I was home playing a 45-rpm vinyl record favorite, so he took off on his bicycle. A short time after he left, the phone rang. I was in my room, so I didn't hear my mother answer. But there suddenly arose frantic calls to hurry and, "Come on." My little brother and sister were already in the car by the time I reached the back door, and I remember repeating, "What's the matter, what's going on," but my mom kept rushing.

"Let's go, get in the car!" In no time, we were down the block and she was out of the car. We were commanded to stay, but I squirmed to get a look and sense of what was happening; I studied expressions, strained to hear conversations, examined subdued bystanders, and worriedly grew concerned at my mother's demeanor. Suddenly, the group along the curb where my mom stood shifted position slightly, and there it was: The crumpled bicycle laying at the street's edge. My heart sank in frozen reality.

My mother's return to the car seemed to be in somber, slow-motion; or maybe it was shock. As, she sat behind the driver's seat, her head lowered. I remember her faint voice: "There's been an accident; we're going to the hospital."

2
THE THREAT

Today, much of the religious world enjoys a recommitment to faith and the Bible. But there are dangerous forces advancing an agenda which threatens biblical teachings and the family. For years, there has been an escalating effort to chip away at the Judeo-Christian foundation of the United States to rewrite American history and erase its culture and divide its citizenry. The eventual  goal is the collapse of the United States Constitution, destruction of a civil union, and, ultimately, the end of its sovereignty and dominance as a source of goodness and power in the defense of liberty and as a beacon of light and hope to millions around the world. History has demonstrated tyrannical powers demand supreme allegiance to their regimes; they do not tolerate devotion to a higher power or to a functional, cohesive family unit where children are loved and are influenced by parents, grandparents, worship services, religious communities, and the Scriptures. To effectively accomplish the fall of a free society and the rise of an oppressive dictatorship, suppression of religious freedom and the destruction of the family are paramount.

Vladimir Lenin was a Russian revolutionary leader who declared, "Give me two generations of children of Americans in school without

God and I will take the nation without firing a shot!"[9] He once stated, "A lie told often enough becomes the truth." He also declared, "It is true that liberty is precious—so precious that it must be rationed" and, "The goal of Socialism is Communism."[10] " Nikita Khrushchev, the Soviet Union leader during the Cold War, boasted, "I can prophesy that your grandchildren in America will live under socialism—our firm conviction is that, sooner or later, Capitalism will give way to Socialism. Whether you like it or not, history is on our side. We will bury you."[11] "Your children's children will live under Communism. You Americans are so gullible. No, you won't accept Communism outright; but we'll keep feeding you small doses of Socialism until you will finally wake up and find that you already have Communism. We won't have to fight you; we'll so weaken your economy, until you fall like overripe fruit into our hands."[12]

Joseph Stalin's own abusive and dysfunctional family may have contributed to his rebellion against the Greek Orthodoxy roots of his childhood and to his decision to become a religion-persecuting atheist. He was a Marxist with a philosophical justification that allowed the killing of millions of Russians. He adopted the Communist Party's stance that claimed religion damaged his perfect communist society and he followed in Lenin's tradition of indoctrinated atheism in all State schools. He initiated a nationwide campaign to destroy churches, seize or destroy church property, and persecute and kill church officials.[13] It has been said Stalin remains one of the greatest villains of the 20th century. Joseph Stalin's forced industrialization of the Soviet Union caused the worst man-made famine in human history.[14] Some sources claim deaths from his massive extinction of humanity range from 6 to 9 million,[15] but others put the death toll much higher.[16]

Mussolini was originally a socialist, who then turned to fascism. He was an avowed atheist but acknowledged the Catholic Church had expansive influence world-wide, so he wore the Catholic disguise because it advanced his political agenda. He likened his fascism to a religion, saying, "The keystone of the fascist doctrine is its conception of the State, of its essence, its functions, and its aims. For Fascism, the State is absolute, individuals and groups relative."[17] Hitler used him during the war to advance his persecution of the Jews.

Initially, Hitler played a political game with the Christian church for his own gain but eventually his game turned into a brutal assault. The Catholic Church denounced Hitler's Party and his ideology, so a *concordat* with the Church was negotiated under the guise of religious protection. The document guaranteed "the property and activities of those Catholic organizations and the associations whose aims are purely religious, cultural, or charitable . . . will be protected." But the article did not define "purely religious," so the Nazi's ended up using the loose language to their advantage and ultimately the *Reich Concordant* severely restricted the Church's ability to resist the Nazi government.[18]

Hitler's designs were similar for the Protestants, as he planned to take control of the newly organized German Evangelical Church and turn it into an arm piece of the Nazi party. However, there was much internal struggle within the Church, as elements of Christianity battled Nazi ideology. Hitler eventually realized the German Evangelical Church would never be the useful puppet he intended to serve his political needs, so the Nazi party doubled-down with its propaganda against churches and Hitler became successful in eventually depriving them of their political power. The Nazi's would then rule with military might and its ideology would be forced upon the families of Germany. It was time to rid the country of all Jews and

to purge the SS (Schutzstaffel) and German society of any Christian elements. All religious educational institutions were converted into secular facilities and all religious symbols were banished. State legislation was implemented and enforced to prevent any resistance to it by the churches.[19]

The Nazi's then targeted impressionable youths who would no longer be "plagued" with objectionable religious influences. Whereas parents and religious discipline once helped shape their young minds and prepared them with ballooning hopes of a promising future that led to the achievement of their own noble dreams, Hitler's new Germany succeeded in propelling a whole generation, deceived by a depraved reverie of the superior utopia, into reckless abandonment of any boundaries of human decency.

Once political dominance had been achieved, Hitler relentlessly pursued the elimination of Christianity from Germany and his atheistic riddance continued until the end of World War II. By the time the terror ended, the Nazis had killed nearly 6 million Jews and millions of sympathizers. Finally, with the fall of the Third Reich, any remaining underground-Christians, and other persecuted resisters, were left with the seemingly insurmountable task of picking up the shattered pieces of their German culture and rebuilding the name and reputation of their country.[20]

♫ BALLOONS

Hurry up; don't go so slow, I can't keep up ahead
They won't wait for me, even if I run
All the world is racing, I don't think I'll get it done
Hurry, don't let go of my hand, I don't want to fail
My dreams are grand!

Today is yours, Tomorrow will be mine
Will I be ready in time
I'll be there for you, if you are here for me
Show me how to rope the moon
That sky looks high and free
Hurry, don't let go of my hand
Release your colored balls - balloons are grand!

I can be an architect. No, I think I'll be a star!
Wait, I could build a rocket and set records out on Mars
Never mind. I should cure a cancer
Or help Grandpa hear out loud ♪
Well actually, I'll be first to college
And make Mom and Dad real proud

Hurry fast, don't go so slow, I must keep up ahead
They're expecting me so, we will have to run
All the world is racing, time to rush to get it done
Hurry, take hold of mine hand, I don't want to fail ♫
My dreams are grand
Hurry, can you please lend me a hand, I don't want to fail
Balloons are grand!

I, too, recall grand childhood dreams, but I was a ten-year-old
when my idyllic life ended. We were never told the name of the
teenager who drove the car that hit my brother on his bicycle. He
had been speeding down a sleepy residential street but, tragically,
his life, as he knew it, ended that day too. He would forever carry
the painful burden of skidding into a child on a bike. Although my
brother physically survived, I really lost him in a fateful moment.
He returned several days later from a hospitalized concussion and
coma. I was so thrilled to see him. I wanted to run to hug him and
shout cheers of joy for his return. But we were told to be careful and
quiet. I did not know the extent of neurologic damage yet—no one
did. But manifestations soon appeared to indicate that the changing
leaves of his young life were beginning to fall on the barren ground
of an unforgiving frost.

3
THE COVENANT

T here are many Judeo-Christian cultural elements that differ from Middle Eastern ones, which contribute to the East/ West clash of civilizations. Such differences, including any grievances between cultures, have magnified, and intensified for thousands of years. But the primary underlying conflict is one that arises out of a complete misunderstanding of Abraham's Covenant. Extremist individuals in the Middle East have erroneously believed all these centuries if the children of Israel could be eliminated (as well as, their supporters), all the blessings of Abraham's Covenant would rightly be theirs. Israel has no right to exist because they believe their own rightful blessings were fraudulently usurped or stolen. As descendants of Ishmael (Abraham's first child), they think they were entitled to the promises made by the Lord to Abraham. But, tragically, their intentions are misguided because they confuse a covenant with a birthright, and they misunderstand God's covenantal relationship with Sarah and Abraham. A covenant is an agreement entered in to voluntarily by two or more parties. Biblically, a covenant is the agreement or engagement of God with man, as revealed in Scripture. In contrast,

the birthright is an inheritance or right of the firstborn, often involving land and authority.

Within the Church of Jesus Christ of Latter-day Saints, Abraham's Covenant, or the Abrahamic Covenant, is also known as The Gospel Covenant. It is important to understand the meaning of this Covenant and, especially, its significance in today's environment as it relates to the family and to God's covenantal relationship with mankind. Therefore, a review of Abraham's covenant in the Scriptures continues.

Genesis 17 records the covenant the Lord made with Abraham. "And when Abram was ninety years old and nine, the Lord appeared to Abram and said unto him, I am the Almighty God; walk before me and be thou perfect. And I will make my covenant between me and thee and will multiply thee exceedingly" Gen. 17:1-2 (KJV). "At this, Abram fell face down on the ground. Then God said to him, this is my covenant with you: I will make you the father of a multitude of nations. What's more, I am changing your name. It will no longer be Abram. Instead you will be called Abraham, for you will be the father of many nations" Gen. 17:3-5 (NLT).

The Lord changed his name to Abraham to symbolize the covenant made between them, representing the "new" and improved person of God he would become, owing to his holy recommitment to the Lord. God continued, "And I will make you extremely fruitful; your descendants will become many nations, and kings will be among them" Gen. 17:6 (NLT). "And I will establish my covenant between me and thee and thy seed after thee in their generations for an everlasting covenant, to be a God unto thee and to thy seed after thee." And I will give unto thee, and to thy seed after thee, the land wherein thou art a stranger, all the land of Canaan, for an everlasting possession; and I will be their God" Gen. 17:7-8 (KJV).

The Church of Jesus Christ of Latter-day Saints is founded upon a restoration of biblical doctrines that were lost or altered due to translation errors, misinterpretation and/or errors of omission. The latter-day Church of Jesus Christ, organized and replicated after Jesus Christ's Church in His day, with a prophet and apostles, depends upon revealed scripture to restore and enhance understanding of biblical teachings. It also relies on inspired guidance to direct the personal and societal challenges that confront modern civilization.

With the restoration of revealed scripture, in addition to biblical scripture, it is understood that Abraham was promised, through his covenant with the Lord, an everlasting seed (an eternal family), a promised land (now and hereafter), and everything in the Father's kingdom, through the ordinances of the Gospel/Priesthood: "And he that receiveth my Father receiveth my Father's kingdom; therefore, all that my Father hath shall be given unto him;"[21] And, "In my Father's house are many mansions . . . I go there to prepare a place for you. And if I go and prepare a place for you, I will come again, and receive you unto myself; that where I am, there you may be also" John 14:2-3 (KJV).

The Lord then told Abraham that his wife was included within the covenant. "Then God said unto Abraham, "Regarding Sarai, your wife—her name will no longer be Sarai. From now on, her name will be Sarah. And I will bless her and give you a son from her! Yes, I will bless her richly, and she will become the mother of many nations. Kings of nations will be among her descendants" Gen.17:15-16 (NLT). Her name change was also the symbol of her covenant with and her holy recommitment to the Lord. Abraham was told their son would be named Isaac, and he would be born (into this covenantal relationship) within the next year: ". . . my covenant I will establish with Isaac, which Sarah will bear unto you at this set time in the next year" Gen. 17:21 (KJV).

Genesis 17 records how Abraham worried about Ishmael. "So, Abraham said to God, 'May Ishmael live under your special blessing?' Gen. 17:18 (NLT). And God said, 'No—Sarah, your wife, will give birth to a son for you; you will name him Isaac; and I will confirm my covenant with him and his descendants as an everlasting covenant. And as for Ishmael, I will bless him also, just as you have asked. I will make him extremely fruitful and multiply his descendants. He will become the father of twelve princes, and I will make him a great nation'" Gen. 17:19-20 (NLT). "*But my covenant will I establish with Isaac, which Sarah will bear to thee at this set time in the next year*" Gen. 17:21 (KJV).

Sarah understood she was the other half of the everlasting covenant Abraham made with the Lord. (Technically, Sarah and Abraham were part of a three-way covenant between God and themselves). When Isaac was born, she said to Abraham, "...Cast out this bondwoman and her son; for the son of the bondwoman shall not be heir with my son, even with Isaac" Gen. 21:10 (KJV). Abraham again worried about Ishmael, "And God said to him, 'Do not be so distressed about the boy . . . listen to whatever Sarah tells you, because it is through Isaac that your offspring will be reckoned'" Gen. 21:12 (NLT).

So, Abraham sent Hagar and her son away. She wandered in the wilderness, and after using up all the water in her canister, Hagar sat under a bush and cried because she couldn't bear to see the death of her child. God heard her cries and sent an angel to comfort her. The scriptures recorded, "And Abraham rose up early in the morning, and took bread, and a bottle of water, and gave it unto Hagar, putting it on her shoulder, and the child, and sent her away, and she departed and wandered in the wilderness . . . When the water was spent in the bottle, she cast the child under one of the shrubs. And she went

and sat down over against him a good way off . . . for she said, let me not see the death of the child. And she . . . lifted up her voice and wept. And God heard . . . Gen. 21:14-17 (KJV).

An angel called to Hagar, telling her not to be afraid. He said he would bless her son's posterity and they would become a great nation. Eventually, the angel led her to safety. ". . . And the angel of God called to Hagar out of heaven, and said unto her, What aileth thee, Hagar? Fear not; for God hath heard the voice of the lad . . . Arise, lift up the lad, and hold him in thine hand; for I will make him a great nation. And God opened her eyes and she saw a well of water; and she went and filled the bottle with water and gave the lad drink . . ." Gen. 21:17-19 (KJV). Hagar did not return to Abraham's household because Isaac was to be raised as the sole heir of the Covenant. "And Abraham gave all that he had unto Isaac. But unto the sons of the concubines. . . Abraham gave gifts, and sent them away from Isaac, his son . . ." Gen. 25:5-6 (KJV).

Ishmael was not a part of the everlasting covenant because he was not born into the family of Sarah and Abraham, the covenantal couple. Rather, God blessed Ishmael with a temporal gift because He seemed to comfort Abraham in his love for this child. It was promised that Ishmael would be made fruitful and would have his numbers greatly increased; he would be the father of twelve princes, and his would be a *great* nation (as recorded in Genesis 17:20). In this verse of the Hebrew Bible, the word for *great*, "gadol" (לודג), most commonly references size, and translates as "large in magnitude, number and/or intensity." Additionally, the word could imply power and importance.[22]

The *everlasting* blessings of the covenant, however, are *inherited* through Isaac. All descendants of Sarah and Abraham qualify for these blessings as well as all who are adopted into their family through the Gospel Covenant, or Abraham's Covenant: ". . . for as many as receive this Gospel shall be called after thy name, and shall be accounted thy seed, and shall rise up and bless thee, as their father . . ." Abraham 2:10.[23]

When the Lord told Abraham, ". . . walk before me and be thou perfect, He indicated the everlasting blessings of the Covenant were conditional upon an effort to keep the commandments; they were based upon the principle of righteous aspiration. The first blessing, a spiritual and eternal blessing, was one of an everlasting posterity. Abraham was one hundred years old, and Sarah ninety, when their only child was born. They waited a lifetime for this good fortune, and they understood the promises were preserved only in and through their son, Isaac (by way of their grandson, Jacob, whose name was changed to Israel).

The second blessing was that of a promised land (now and hereafter). "By faith Abraham, when he was called out to go into a place which he should after receive for an inheritance, obeyed; and he went out, not knowing whither he went. By faith he sojourned in the land of promise, as in a strange country, dwelling in tabernacles with Isaac and Jacob, the heirs with him of the same promise" Hebrews 11:8-9

(KJV). "Abraham was confidently looking forward to a city with eternal foundations, a city designed and built by God" Hebrews 11:10 (NLT). "It was by faith even Sarah was able to have a child, though she was barren and was too old. She believed God would keep his promise. And so, a whole nation came from this one man, who was as good as dead—a nation with so many people that, like the stars in the sky and the sand on the seashore, there is no way to count them" Heb. 11:11-12 (NTL). "*. . . These people died still believing what God had promised them. They did not receive what was promised but they saw it all from a distance and welcomed it. They agreed that they were foreigners and nomads here on earth*" Heb 11:13 (NLT).

* * *

Am I a foreigner and nomad here on earth? I remember thoughts like this throughout my adolescence. *And what is the point of it all, anyway?* Characteristic parts of my brother remained, roughly, for the next ten years, but much of his personality was slowly slipping away. He was an amazing talent—a "rock star" at school and in his local band. We were in High School a Capella Choir together, and I accompanied the many productions in which he was a lead singer and prominent performer, including Christmas and Easter concerts, state travelling competitions and collaborations, and school plays and musicals. But his gentle soul and charming charisma were frequently interrupted with angry outbursts and neurological spasms, similar to seizures (but not as severe) and twitches or tremors. I did not comprehend at the time, but with many years of life's experiences, I now wonder if his anger and frustration was not akin to that of those who suffer the deteriorating effects of chronic and debilitating disease or aging. Alzheimer's, Parkinson's, and other conditions can trigger patients to lash out from the awareness they are helplessly losing control and critical components of themselves due to a deterioration of the brain.

Many times, I have reflected on the certain inner turmoil my brother had endure, as he suffered involuntary changes and degenerating motor control, frequently eliciting hostile reactions from teachers, classmates, neighbors, friends, or even *family: And that finger would be pointed at me.* I am embarrassed to confess, I reacted personally to his fits of frustration, defending myself or returning insults for offense. I wish I knew then what my parents knew. They had always reacted with measured patience and compassionate empathy. It was just as painful, confusing, overwhelming, and foreign to them, but they had the parental love and faith-filled maturity to rely on prayer and scripture for coping mechanisms and a Godly perspective.

The childhood faith I had enjoyed from Sunday school songs and Bible stories of Jesus was steadily fading. After the accident and evolving changes, a struggle followed throughout many stolen years as I wrestled pain and battled anger. I undertook a search the world over for answers to explain life's meaning. Even the best journals and resources had none to offer. When the pain became increasingly difficult to manage, I fell prey to the belief there really were no answers or escape from confusion, loss, and suffering.

Life is hard. It drives many to destructive coping mechanisms but, surprisingly, others seem to experience a rebound apparatus that propels them to extraordinary achievements. This was an intriguing mystery to which I found myself drawn. Despite the anguish and despair of loss, a distant memory of hope and optimism often nipped at my heels. *What is the meaning of the Jesus story anyway—the miracles, the cross, the resurrection? I longed for one of those famous New Testament miracles.* Even though my direction was aimless, and my faith waned, eventually, something told me to return to my roots: The Bible.

* * *

When God commanded Abraham to sacrifice Isaac, he understood altogether if Isaac were to die, the everlasting covenant and all the eternal promises contained therein would die with him. If Isaac no longer existed, neither did the everlasting promises. God would cease to be God because God's inherent nature is that of truthfulness. Regardless of the inner turmoil Abraham must have assuredly experienced as he climbed the mount with his only child of promise, his absolute faith in the Lord remained steadfast. Certainly, he wrestled with despair on that arduous trek up the hill, but the Bible tells how he believed God's promise and was reasonably able to imagine, or envision, if he had to sacrifice Isaac, as the Lord had commanded, God must have a plan to raise Isaac from the dead in order to keep His promise in establishing the covenant He had made with him. "By faith Abraham, when God tested him, offered Isaac as a sacrifice. He who had embraced the promises was about to sacrifice his one and only son, even though God had said to him, 'It is through Isaac that your offspring will be reckoned'" Heb. 11:17-18 (NLT). Abraham trusted the Lord would revive Isaac, "Accounting that God was able

to raise him up, even from the dead, from whence he received him in a figure" Heb. 11:19 (KJV). Fortunately for Abraham, an angel intervened and prevented the sacrifice of Isaac. The sacrifice and resurrection of his only begotten son was merely a trial of faith; it was not a reality. By contrast, the story of Abraham and Isaac represents the unmistakable symbolism contained in the actual Sacrifice and Resurrection of God's Only Begotten Son: The Lord and Savior of the World, Jesus Christ.

With the final blessing of the Covenant, the Lord guaranteed Abraham he (by means of his faithful and committed efforts in keeping their covenant) would inherit everything the Father has, through the Priesthood/Gospel. "And, also, all they who receive this priesthood receive me, saith the Lord; For he that receiveth my servants, receiveth me; And he that receiveth me, receiveth my Father; And he that receiveth my Father, receiveth my Father's kingdom; therefore, all that my Father hath shall be given unto him."[24]

These everlasting blessings of Abraham's Covenant are promised to all: Righteous individuals not born into the family of Sarah and Abraham, will have the opportunity to be adopted into it (through commitment to this same Gospel Covenant made with the Lord), by way of their son, Isaac, and their grandson, Jacob, and inherit all the covenantal blessings, through the House of Israel. "And I will bless them through thy name; for as many as receive this Gospel shall be called after thy name, and shall be accounted thy seed, and shall rise up and bless thee, as their father; and I will bless them that bless thee and curse them that curse thee; and in thee (that is, in thy Priesthood) and in thy seed . . . I give unto thee a promise that this right shall continue in thee, and in thy seed after thee (the literal seed of the body) shall all the families of the earth be blessed, even with the blessings of the Gospel, which are the blessings of salvation, even of eternal life" Abraham 2:10-11, (footnote 11*a*, House of *Israel, Blessings of*).[25]

* * *

With winter rapidly approaching, one late-September afternoon, my dad and then-19-year-old brother were rushing to complete the hanging of storm windows, as breezy winds scattered autumn leaves and blew ominous chills through their weary bones. Suddenly, my brother stopped to stare at a neighbor halfway down the block who was working in his yard. He turned and agitatedly said, "Can you believe that? I can't believe what he said. Did you hear that, Dad? You're not going to let him talk about me like that, are you?" My dad was bewildered, "What are you talking about? I can't hear a thing; he's all the way down the street." Slightly wobbling on the ladder, he attempted to hurry him, "Come on, can you just hand me the window?" But my brother's distress increased; fixation gripped and agitated him. He could not refocus but obsessed on his perceived insult. He stood there adamant and troubled, insisting he could not work under such insufferable conditions. Amid worry and confusion, my dad finally climbed down the ladder and put a calming arm on his son's shoulder, then led him away from the unsettling scene, into the security of his own room. There he sat on his bed, staring at the floor. My mom, who had followed as they entered, anxiously searched my dad's face for some indication of answers or explanation for my brother's troubled demeanor. But there was none.

Many episodes of his confusion, delusion, hallucinations, and fear would follow, but the heartbreaking truth would eventually be confirmed in a diagnosis of paranoid schizophrenia. Throughout several following years, there was ignorance, uncertainty, desperation, denial, research, prayers, hope, despair, recognition, admission, concession, and resignation. Eventually, the black cloud of finality descended on the storm-wrecked aftermath, only to lament the tale of our adored son, brother, cousin, friend, and majestic talent who had once been known for too short a time. It felt to me like these prayers were never destined to permeate an impenetrable ceiling.

A Better Friend ♫

Life's been good; yea, life's been great, Although there's no
    escaping fate
Your arrival in my life became, Fulfillment of my childish game
But when I turned my back to play, you slipped outside the
    backyard gate
Then never to return again, you taunt and tease what might
    have been

Wish I had been a better friend, the short time that I knew
    you when
Wish I had been that kind of friend, on whom you knew
    you could depend
If only now my notes could break through scrambled tunes
    you can't escape
If only love could penetrate the troubled symphony that plays

I hear your golden voice sublime while thinking back to
wistful times
When solos, duos, trios sang of hopes and fears, of joys
and pangs
Remember when the world was ours, A future filled with
hearts and flowers
I still see stars for you and me that skim the sky eternally

Life's been good; rather, life's been great, although a piece is
missing straight
To fairy tales that end with joy, For every mother's girl and boy
Where did you go? When will you come to hear my
ever-constant drum
Would that you could return again and capture just what
might have been!

Wish I had been a better friend, the short time that I knew
you when
Wish I had been that kind of friend, on whom you knew
you could depend
If only now my notes could break through scrambled tunes
you can't equate
If only love could penetrate that sleeping symphony that waits

4
THE COUPLE

To further assist in the understanding of the everlasting covenant in the book of Matthew in the Bible, there is an exchange between Jesus and the Sadducees. The Sadducees were an aristocracy of leadership who opposed Jesus for his cleansing of the temple, which they regarded as an infringement of their rights.[26] They didn't believe in the resurrection but asked a question about marriage in the resurrection, with the intent to stump Jesus. "That same day Jesus was approached by some Sadducees—religious leaders who say there is no resurrection from the dead. They posed this question: 'Teacher, Moses said if a man dies without having children, his brother should marry the widow and have a child who will carry on the brother's name. Well... there were seven brothers. The oldest one married and then died without children, so his brother married the widow. But the second brother also died, and the third brother married her. This continued with all seven of them. Last of all, the woman also died. So, tell us whose wife will she be in the resurrection? For all seven were married to her.' Jesus replied, 'Your mistake is that you don't know the scriptures and you don't know the power of God'" Matt. 22:23-29 (NLT). "'For in the resurrection, they neither marry nor are given in marriage but are as the angels of God in heaven.'" "'But as touching (upon) the resurrection of the dead— have you not read that which was spoken unto you by God, saying: 'I am the God of Abraham, and the God of Isaac, and the God of

Jacob? . . .'" Matt. 22:30-32 (KJV). "(Jesus said) '. . . God is not the God of the dead, but of the living'" Matt. 22:32 (KJV). "And when the crowds heard this, they were aston-ished at his teaching" Matt. 22:33 (NLT).

As was typical of Jesus, the Master Teacher, his answer astounded them. His response referenced the biblical doctrine of Abraham's Covenant, the everlasting covenant. He chastised them, noting they didn't understand the scriptures, nor did they believe the power of God unto the fulfillment of them. Abraham's Covenant is the covenant all human beings will make individually with the Lord, so they may receive the same promises guaranteed to Sarah and Abraham. The everlasting blessings of the covenant are conditional upon a righteous endeavor to adhere to the command-ments of God. The Gospel covenant begins with faith, repentance, baptism, receiving the Holy Spirit into their lives, and is followed by additional personal covenants, culminating with the *eternal marriage* covenant in the temple, which binds, or seals families together forever. These holy ceremonies (called ordinances) in which covenants are made, must be performed in mortality. They cannot be performed after the final resurrection; Jesus indicated by then, it would be too late because then there will be no marrying, nor giving in mar-riage. This earth is the place and time to form lasting relationships, friendships, and to have families. In the example of the continuously widowed woman in Matthew's account, not one of the marriages was a covenantal marriage; no *everlasting marriage* ordinance had been performed. She was not able to make that covenant in mortality, which would have secured for her the same everlasting blessings of an eternal marriage and family, a promised land, and all that the Lord's kingdom offers—just as Sarah and Abraham. But did this mean the woman would be left out of the everlasting covenant for eternity?

Fortunately for the woman, the all-knowing, all-loving, all-powerful God has thought of an eternal plan of happiness that extends to all His children. Allowances have been made in His Plan for those who did not receive these covenantal ordinances during their lifetimes. All God's children will have the opportunity for these ordinations to be completed, if they so desire. Some good people may not choose this Covenant and, as Jesus said, they will be "*as* the angels of God in heaven." Everyone will be given the option to decide for him or herself. No one will be excluded, and no one will be overlooked. All will be given the choice whether they want to inherit the same covenantal promises as Sarah and Abraham.

Heaven gazing can reveal a breathtaking view of shimmering star clusters, each twinkling its own dance, or of a full-moonlit sky, silhouetting the midnight calm after the distant daily rush, or of the brilliant noonday sun, aglow in the exhilarating warmth of countless golden rays. Each heavenly experience is a unique gift, and each is beautiful and glorious in its own degree. Similarly, God has an eternal reward for all inhabitants of this world, one that is beautiful and glorious, as is a heaven of stars, or moon, or sun. Just *as* the angels in heaven are jubilant in their praise of God, every individual will be jubilant in his or her praise of him for the heavenly reward they receive, as a result of his love for them and his righteous judgements. For those desiring to make covenants with God, they will receive the same promises as Sarah and Abraham. Even though life can be complicated, and possibly messy at times, as it was for the woman with seven husbands, an everlasting true love is the design of a human heart, and the Lord's covenants provide the means to fulfill such a desire.

♫ ON YOUR SIDE

I am on your side; I am all around you
You are on the way now that I have found you
We know what to do, Dance up the clouds into the sun
Aiming bright and clear, for you and me, we are "the one"

I am on your side, I can feel the glory
We hold all the keys, we will turn the story
Eagles soaring high up in the sky, they fly on wings of prayer
Keeping dreams alive within our sight because we dared

No more lonely mountain shadowing the sea, the light
    breaks free
It's radiance beams into the dawn, reflecting it along for all
    eternity
I am on your side, I am all around you, You and I belong
There's nothing now we can't do
Echoes in the breeze, Vows so complete ♫
Now hold on tight and run, Singing bright and clear
This time is ours, we are "the one"

5

THE PLAN

In Moses 1:39, the entire purpose of the whole human existence is revealed: "For behold, this is my work and my glory—to bring to pass the immortality and eternal life of man."[27] And, "Behold I will send you Elijah, the prophet, before the great and dreadful day of the Lord; and he shall turn the heart of the fathers to their children, and the heart of the children to their fathers, lest I come and smite the earth with a curse" Malachi 4:5-6 (KJV). In the Doctrine & Covenants, further clarification of Malachi's prophecy states, "The Prophet Elijah was to plant in the hearts of the children the promises made to their fathers . . . lest the whole earth be smitten with a curse and utterly wasted at his (Christ's) (2nd) coming."[28] The temple responsibility (covenantal ceremonies/ordinances) is part of this earthly ministry and preparation, and must be completed on earth. "And I will give you the keys of the kingdom of heaven, and whatsoever thou shalt bind on earth shall be bound in heaven, and whatsoever thou shalt loose on earth shall be loosed in heaven" Matt 16:19 (KJV).

In the magnificent wisdom and infinite love of the Lord, *all God's children* (who have ever lived or ever will live on the earth) *will have the opportunity* to make his/her own covenants and receive the promised blessings. The woman in the account of Matthew 22, along with the love of her life, will have the same opportunity, just as Sarah and Abraham had had, to covenant with God and receive the promised blessings of an eternal marriage and family, a promised land, and all things in the kingdom of God. These loving relationships she had formed in mortality with her children and others will continue forever. As the Apostle Paul asked in the New Testament, "If the dead will not be raised, what point is there in people being baptized for those who are dead? Why do it unless the dead will someday rise again?" 1Cor. 15:29 (NLT).

This is a glorious promise for everyone, even today. In the temples of the Church of Jesus Christ of Latter-day Saints, sealing ordinances are performed exactly as Paul described to the Corinthians—through proxy substitutions (for the dead). If people do not have the opportunity during their lifetime, and if they do not have any temple-attending descendants, relatives, or friends who could perform these ordinances for them, then the Lord, himself, will oversee the completion of these covenants during the Millennial Reign (a thousand-year period), which will begin at his second coming. Christ instructs all to complete these ordinances, which are reminders of recommitments to God, and are symbolic of the cleansing and sanctification (required to return to God's presence) made possible *only* through His Atoning Sacrifice. All individuals covenanting with God have the opportunity, as well, to complete unfulfilled goals and desires during his

Millennial Reign, such as an unrealized marriage or the raising of a prematurely deceased child.

Jesus' statement, "God is not the God of the dead, but of the living," is an astonishing reinforcement of the reality of the resurrection and of the doctrine of the eternal family. At the time Jesus spoke those words to the Sadducees, Abraham, Isaac, and Jacob were already dead. Yet, He pronounced that He was not the God of the dead but of the living, validating that they *do* live on in the resurrection, as *do* the promises made to them.

* * *

There were many nudges and promptings that enticed me to revisit my childhood fondness and familiarity with the Scriptures. It took many years of research and study for me to begin putting the scattered pieces of Biblical truths together but, eventually, the puzzle of Sarah and Abraham's covenant with God began to reveal itself. The hopelessness and pain of losing the brother I once knew finally began taking a turnaround towards awe-struck amazement that God, in his Omni-benevolence, had devised such a wondrous plan which could rectify the sorrow and disappointment experienced in mortality. When I finally began to realize the profound significance of Christ's atonement and resurrection, I remember my heart leaping with joy, in anticipation for a glorious and jubilant reunion with that enchanting sibling of my youth, unmarred by the afflictions of his accident and bound to our eternal family forever.

* * *

Often throughout Scripture, when there were no temples on the earth, the Lord used a mountain to accomplish his holy purposes. The most recognizable example of this is in, Exodus 24:12 (KJV), when God delivered the Ten Commandments to Moses. "And the Lord said unto Moses, 'Come up to me into the mount, and be there: And I will give thee tablets of stone, and a law, and commandments which I have written; that thou mayest teach them.'"

God's perfect plan to teach the commandments and make covenants with his children would have been fatally flawed if there had been no accommodation for the mistakes and limitations of man. When God commanded Abraham to ". . . walk before me and be thou perfect," He clearly knew the impossibility of perfection within the fallen state of mortality. But there was an accommodation, which the Savior, Jesus Christ, would make for the world. At the end of his earthly ministry, the Son of God, a Perfect and Selfless being, would provide an atonement for the sins of mankind, and his Resurrection would break the bands of death, reuniting the body with the spirit, providing the assurance of immortality, and offering eternal life for all.

The Bible declares all are saved by the grace of Jesus Christ. A lifetime of good works cannot get one into the kingdom of God; it is Christ's atonement, through his grace, which allows a return to God. He is known as The God of Heaven and Earth, The Great Mediator, The Advocate with The Father, Our Access into Heaven. The Bible states all humanity is fallen and in need of God's grace to redeem them: "But the scripture hath concluded all under sin, that the promise by faith of Jesus Christ might be given to them that believe" Galatians 3:22 (KJV). The Apostle Paul spoke to the disciples who previously kept the Law of Moses before the coming of Christ: "But before faith came, we were kept under the law, shut up unto the faith which should afterwards be revealed" Galatians 3:23 (KJV).

Paul referred to those outward ceremonies (ordinances), rituals, and symbols of the Law of Moses and likened them to that of a teacher: "Wherefore the law was our schoolmaster to bring us unto Christ, that we might be justified by faith. But after that faith is come, we are no longer under a schoolmaster. For ye are all the children of God, by faith in Christ Jesus" Galatians 3:24-26 (KJV). The ordinances and symbols of the Mosaic Law were preparatory and were given to the children of Israel with the intent of pointing them towards the coming of the Messiah. These rituals were to remind them frequently of their duties and responsibilities to God, as they looked forward to his coming. For example, they were commanded to sacrifice unblemished animals in their offerings. When God instituted the Passover, it was the blood of an unblemished male lamb, placed on the two side posts and upper post of the door that spared the lives of the Israelites' firstborn, as the destroying angel passed by them. The children of Israel had been in bondage and God had sent a series of plagues to their captors as a warning to set them free. But when all warnings went unheeded, He executed judgement, and the final plague was the death of all the families' firstborn throughout the land. After God spared the lives of the Israelites' firstborn and delivered his people, they were then instructed to keep the Passover annually, as a memorial feast throughout the generations. This ordinance is a continual reminder that it was He who had saved their lives and set them free.

With the Mortal Ministry of Jesus Christ came the higher spiritual law—an introspective law of faith, repentance, and ordinances symbolic of spiritual cleansing and sanctification required for salvation, and necessary for a purified return to the presence of the Almighty God. This cleansing and sanctification would come in and through the atonement of Jesus Christ, who was the only unblemished, perfect individual and whose sacrificial, holy blood was able to provide restitution for, and salvation of, this fallen and imperfect world of human beings.

OH, REMEMBER ♫

Oh, remember God saved from Noah's flood
Rainbow symbols convey from up above
That the greatest reward descends on God's priceless friends
    who follow Him And obey their Lord Beloved

Don't forget Abe and Sarah's covenant, Eternal couples, alike,
    all blessings won
The grand Gospel of love sent God from heaven above
With tender grace for all our human family

Oh, remember the God of Abraham, Isaac, Jacob and Israel's
    scattered clan
Like a hen folds her chicks in wing our Savior calls choice
    offspring
Restoring lost favors from his hand

Don't forget Abe and Sarah's covenant, Eternal couples, alike,
    all blessings won
The grand Gospel of love sent God from heaven above
With tender grace for all our human family

Oh, remember God's pact with you and me
All He asks is be faithful and believe
So, remember the promises then just do your very best ♪
A mansion awaits eternally

Don't forget Abe and Sarah's covenant, Eternal couples, alike,
    all blessings won
The grand Gospel of love sent God from heaven above
With tender grace for all our human family

6

THE DREAMS

The account of Jacob's son, Joseph, is a similar example of faith and commitment to God's commands, as was Abraham's example (his great grandfather). Throughout his many trials, Joseph remained devoted to the will of God and to his divine plan for him, not knowing ahead of time exactly what the details of that plan would be. Joseph's family was afflicted by unimaginable dysfunction. His half-brothers hated him because of his flamboyance and his annoying dreams, and because his father adored him. Joseph's mother, Rachael, was the love of Jacob's life, but she died giving birth to his younger brother, Benjamin. Jacob clearly favored them, and his half-brothers resented it. When Joseph conveyed a dream to them in which his stalks of grain stood upright but the brothers' stalks bowed down to him, their tolerance of him finally came to an end, and they conspired to kill him. After leaving him for dead in a deep pit, Judah convinced them to spare his life, instead, by selling him to passing merchants. They stripped him of his elaborate coat of many colors, shredded it, and sold him into Egypt (for twenty pieces of silver.) They killed a goat, covering Joseph's coat in blood, and returned to their devastated father with a tale he had been devoured by a wild beast.

But God was with Joseph in his journeys and afflictions. His talents and charms ushered him into Potiphar's household, where he found himself ruler over all the servants. Genesis 39:2,6 (KJV) states, "And the Lord was with Joseph and he was a prosperous man; and he was in the house of his master, the Egyptian . . . and Joseph was a goodly person, and well favoured."

When Joseph refused the advances of Potiphar's wife, her retaliation of false assault charges landed him in prison. God was still with him, however, and Joseph gained a supervisorial position in the prison. "And Potiphar's wife soon began to look at him lustfully. 'Come and sleep with me,' she demanded. But Joseph refused. 'Look,' he told her, 'my master trusts me with everything in his entire household. No one here has more authority than I do. He has held back nothing from me, except you, because you are his wife. How could I do such a wicked thing? It would be a great sin against God.' She kept putting pressure on Joseph day after day, but he refused to sleep with her, and he kept out of her way as much as possible" Gen. 39:7-10 (NLT).

"One day, however, no one else was around when he went in to do his work. She came and grabbed him by his cloak, demanding, 'Come on, sleep with me!' Joseph tore himself away, but he left his cloak in her hand as he ran from the house. When she saw that she was holding his cloak and he had fled, she called out to her servants. 'Look,' she said, 'My husband has brought this Hebrew slave here to make fools of us! He came to my room to rape me, but I screamed. When he heard me scream, he ran outside and got away, but he left his cloak behind with me.' She kept the cloak with her until her husband came home. Then she told him her story. 'That Hebrew slave you've brought into our house tried to come in and fool around with me,' she said. 'But when I screamed, he ran outside, leaving his cloak with me'" Gen. 39:11-15 (NLT).

"Potiphar was furious when he heard his wife's story about how Joseph had allegedly treated her. So, he took Joseph and threw him into the prison where the king's prisoners were held, and there he remained. But the Lord was with Joseph in the prison and showed him His faithful love. And the Lord made Joseph a favorite with the prison warden. Before long, the warden put Joseph in charge of all the other prisoners and over everything that happened in the prison. The warden had no more worries because Joseph took care of everything. The Lord was with him and caused everything he did to succeed" Gen. 39:19-23 (NLT).

In prison, Joseph accurately interpreted the dreams of the king's (Pharaoh's) chief butler. "And the chief butler told his dream to Joseph and said unto him, 'In my dream behold a vine was before me'" Gen. 40:9 (KJV). "'The vine had three branches that began to bud and blossom, and soon it produced clusters of ripe grapes. I was holding Pharaoh's wine cup in my hand, so I took a cluster of grapes and squeezed the juice into the cup. Then I placed the cup in Pharaoh's hand.' 'This is what the dream means,' Joseph said. 'The three branches represent three days. Within three days Pharaoh will lift you up and restore you to your position as his chief cupbearer (butler). And please remember me and do me a favor when things go well for you. Mention

me to Pharaoh, so he might let me out of this place" Gen. 40:10-14 (NLT). "'For indeed I was stolen away out of the land of the Hebrews; and here also have I done nothing that they should put me into the dungeon'" Gen. 40:15 (KJV).

When the chief cupbearer was restored to his position, he forgot about Joseph, where he remained in prison another two years. "Pharaoh's birthday came three days later, and he prepared a banquet for all his officials and staff . . . he then restored the chief cupbearer to his former position . . . Pharaoh's chief cupbearer, however, forgot all about Joseph, never giving him another thought" Gen. 40:20-21, 23 (NLT).

Two years later, when Pharaoh dreamed of the cattle and the corn, suddenly the butler remembered Joseph in prison. "Two full years later, Pharaoh dreamed that he was standing on the banks of the Nile River. In his dream he saw seven fat, healthy cows come up out of the river and begin grazing in the marsh grass. Then he saw seven more cows come up behind them from the Nile, but these were scrawny and thin. These cows stood beside the fat cows on the riverbank. Then the scrawny, thin cows ate the seven healthy cows! At this point . . . Pharaoh woke up" Gen. 41:1-4 (NLT).

"But he fell asleep again and had a second dream. This time he saw seven heads of grain, plump and beautiful, growing on a single stalk. Then seven more heads of grain appeared, but these were shriveled and withered by the east wind. And these thin heads swallowed up the seven plump and well-formed heads. Then Pharaoh woke up and realized it was a dream" Gen. 41:5-7 (NLT).

"The next morning Pharaoh was very disturbed by the dreams. So, he called for all the magicians and wise men of Egypt . . . not one could tell him what they meant. Finally, the king's chief cupbearer spoke up. 'Today I am reminded of my failure,' he told Pharaoh" Gen. 41:8-9 (NLT). "'There was . . . an Hebrew . . . and he interpreted to us our dreams.' Then Pharaoh sent and called Joseph, and they brought him hastily out of the dungeon" Gen. 41:12,14 (KJV). Joseph interpreted Pharaoh's dreams as seven years of plenty and seven years of famine. He proposed a grain storage program and Pharaoh made him ruler over all Egypt. He was able to sell grain during the famine, saving the lives of the Egyptians and others throughout all the land, among them, his father's family in the land of Canaan.[29]

As a result of the famine, when Jacob's family ran out of food, he sent his sons to Egypt to buy grain, but he refused to send the young Benjamin, terrified he might lose him, too. Joseph was the governor of the land, so the brothers presented him with their grain request, bowing to him, as he had envisioned in his dream years ago. He knew them immediately, but they did not recognize the grown adult who stood before them, so he plotted to learn the condition of his father and brother. He accused them of being spies. They denied it, saying they were a large family in need of food. He asked for more details regarding this large family, concocting the scheme to see his father and brother again. He commanded the guards to seize the older brother, as hostage, to ensure their return, and to prove they were not spies. Then he sent them with money and a small food portion, anxiously awaiting the return with his younger brother, for the remainder of grain. Distraught, they journeyed back to relay Joseph's demands to their horrified father.

After initial refusal and much distress, Jacob finally relented to allow the return to Egypt, weeping and bidding goodbye to his beloved Benjamin. Upon return, Joseph laid eyes on his young brother and excused himself to privately cry for joy. He then prepared them a grand feast and watched from his chambers, as they dined. After they ate and drank, preparations were made to return home and they set off on their journey. But the drama continued, with Joseph creating more intrigue, although, eventually he revealed his identity to his brothers. When they realized he was not dead but was the architect of the storage plan which spared the entire land from death, they were grieved and troubled at their past transgressions. "Please come closer . . . I am Joseph, your brother, whom you sold into slavery in Egypt! But don't be upset and don't be angry with yourselves for selling me to this place. It was God who sent me here ahead of you to preserve your lives. This famine that has ravaged the land for two years will last five more years, and there will be neither plowing nor harvesting" Gen. 45:4-6 (NLT). "And God sent me before you to preserve you a posterity in the earth and to save your lives by a great deliverance. So, it was not you that sent me hither, but God: And he hath made me a father to Pharaoh, and lord of all his house, and a ruler throughout all the land of Egypt" Gen. 45:7-8 (KJV). "Then his brothers came and threw themselves down before Joseph. 'Look, we are your slaves!' they said. But Joseph replied, 'You intended to harm me, but God intended it all for good. He brought me to this position so I could save the lives of many people'" Gen. 50:18,20 (NLT). Joseph forgave his brothers and relocated his father's family closer to him in Goshen, where Jacob lived until he died. He was then returned to Canaan to be buried with his grandfather, Abraham, and his father, Isaac.

* * *

I've often been asked, "Do you wish you had lost your brother suddenly? Is it harder to lose a loved one gradually, being constantly reminded they really left long ago?" My reply is always a resounding, "No." I am so grateful to have a few substantive components that remain. There are still bits of his entertaining personality that re-surface, albeit in the most unexpected, childish ways and nonsensical moments.

One Christmas Eve, we all sat around the brightly decorated, sparkling tree, watching him open his gifts (and he always expressed gratitude for everything he received, thanking us, and referencing the gift of baby Jesus' birth.) But the envelopes of dollar bills were his favorite gifts. Perhaps they reminded him of his teenage, summer days working in construction. He felt so productive and accomplished, watching his disciplined weekly savings multiply. So, with each opened Christmas envelope of $1 or $2 (his sharp math skills accounting for every increase), his anticipation continued to grow until he could not contain the excitement any longer. Opening the last envelope and clutching the wad of dollars accumulated in his hand, he suddenly sprang out of his chair, hands to the ceiling, and deliriously declared, "Thirty-seven whole dollars! Oh, thank you— God bless the cash!"

While not the most reverent expression of Christmas' true meaning, it has been one of the more enduring memories. And there were many such moments, when the entire room would erupt into outbreaks of laughter and incredulity at his wacky ways. Just as the Biblical saga of Joseph taught many lessons of faith, trust, and perseverance, these many Christmas-like experiences have been instructional reminders to always look for God's purpose in our circumstances (which are often not understood at the time), and appreciate any humor that might be sprinkled among the difficulties of life. And thank God we have been given some remaining moments to cherish with him.

* * *

Through Joseph's devotion and commitment, he recognized God's hand in saving not only his own people from death but all of Egypt and the entire land round about. Once again, the account of Joseph, who was betrayed and sold into Egypt, is yet another unmistakable symbolic representation of the betrayal and sale (for thirty pieces of silver) of our Lord and Savior, Jesus Christ. In the same way Joseph had trusted in God's plan, Christ made no attempt to flee the chief priests or the Roman authorities when he was betrayed. He loved the world so greatly He allowed himself to be led, as a lamb to the slaughter, to willingly accomplish His Father's design: He obediently provided the atonement, which offers forgiveness and salvation ("by a great deliverance") not only for His own people, but for the entire family of man.

After the death of Jesus, his apostles and disciples were confused and despairing. They had believed the prophecies of his coming, and they followed Him throughout his earthly ministry, eagerly attempting to learn truth from his parables and example. But never in the history of the world had there been an atonement nor a resurrection. They did not understand all that he tried to teach them. It wasn't until they encountered two angels after his resurrection that they were reminded of Jesus' words:

"And, behold, there was a man named Joseph, a counsellor; and he was a good man . . . he was of Arimathea, a city of the Jews: Who also himself waited for the kingdom of God. This man went unto Pilate and begged the body of Jesus. And he took it down, and wrapped it in linen, and laid it in a sepulcher…" Luke 23:50-53 (KJV).

"But very early on Sunday morning, the women went to the tomb, taking the spices they had prepared. They found the stone

had been rolled away from the entrance. So, they went in, but they didn't find the body of the Lord Jesus. As they stood there puzzled, two men suddenly appeared to them, clothed in dazzling robes. The women were terrified and bowed with their faces to the ground. Then the men asked, 'Why are you looking among the dead for someone who is alive? He isn't here! He has risen from the dead! Remember what he told you, back in Galilee, that the Son of Man must be betrayed into the hands of sinful men and be crucified, and that he would rise again on the third day'" Luke 24:1-7 (NLT). "And they remembered his words" Luke 24:8 (KJV).

The women at the tomb did not comprehend what had happened on the third day. But many concepts within the Scriptures have now been understood for centuries. Still, it is easy to forget them. We all want to believe the holy words. Intellectually, we do but, emotionally, it is natural to wonder if they truly apply to us. Often, we just feel like giving up amid hopelessness. The verse in, Mark 9:24 (KJV), expressed this best. When a father brought his convulsing son to Jesus, he asked Him to have compassion and bless them with one of his miracles, of which he had heard so many rumors. Jesus told him miracles are possible to those who believe. Then the tearful man cried out, "...I believe; *help thou mine unbelief.*"

This has always been one of my favorite verses because I firmly believe *in* God but, sometimes, I forget to *believe* him when he says miracles are possible. He used miracles in the Bible to teach us of his goodness and power, which is available to those who believe him. He also taught us that the miracle of the Resurrection was in his power. The greatest of all his performed miracles was the raising of the dead to life, symbolizing the gift of immortality everyone receives, through the majesty of His Resurrection. Although our miracles are not always the same as those we recall during his ministry (and usually they don't turn out to be the ones we think we want or need) miracles still occur when we believe and trust God's plan for our lives. This has been a tough life lesson because I have always wanted God to just heal my brother but, evidently, He has a different miracle in mind.

Jeremiah 1:5 (KJV) tells: Before I formed thee in the belly, I knew thee, and before thou camest forth out of the womb, I sanctified thee and I ordained thee a prophet unto the nations." This passage always causes me to reflect on the thought that God knew me (all of us) before we were even born and has a call, a plan, a unique purpose for each life. Don't we all wonder what our purposes are? I have questioned why I am here. Am I such a miserable creature, I needed the refining and humbling opportunities that only come from the loss of a loved one, which should lead me to developing characteristics of hope, faith, patience, kindness, charity, compassion, empathy, sacrifice—to name a few? These traits do not come easily to me, but I have learned more about them from experiences with my brother than I could have ever learned without then. *Would that be the miracle in all of this?*

NON-STOP TO O'HARE ♫

A blanket of white beneath the night, the flickering lights
    must be Cedar Rapids now in sight
The tailwind's strong, it won't be long, *The Jingle Rock* song
    is playing over all along
Ginger boys, bustling noise, hidden toys, Christmas joys
All are waiting for me there with a non-stop to O'Hare

Non-stop to O'Hare always takes me there
Back to the days before, back to the ways before a world of care
Non-stop to O'Hare, always take me there, bring those mem-
    ories clear, chase away the fear, my non-stop to O'Hare

The faces awaiting me, worries abating, the music's creating
    a scene for all the world to share
The mistletoe and mini glows, that rapid pose which only
    Kodac's moment knows
Forget-me-nots, the haven't-gots and Toys for Tots, they need
    us lots
Can't forget the reason ne'er, for the non-stop to O'Hare ♪

Non-stop to O'Hare always takes me there
Back to the days before, back to the ways before a world of care
Non-stop to O'Hare, always take me there, bring those mem-
    ories clear, chase away the fear, my non-stop to O'Hare

The welcoming smile awaiting while we begin to file down
    that long resounding "mile"

The Center cries for smiles and "hi's", Distant, hollow eyes
    reach & plead for loving ties
But Bethlehem bore that Gem, The Hope Emblem, Wondrous
    Diadem
So, book your own resembling fare of a non-stop to O'Hare

Non-stop to O'Hare always takes me there
Back to the days before, back to the ways before a world of
    care ♫
Non-stop to O'Hare, keep my heart aflare, bring those mem-
    ories clear, chase away the fear, my non-stop to O'Hare

7

THE BENEFACTOR

"Grace is when God gives us what we don't deserve, and mercy is when God doesn't give us what we do deserve." ~ Unknown

Critics of the Bible assert the God of the Old Testament is not the same God as that of the New Testament. The Old Testament God was severe and vengeful, while the New Testament God was compassionate and forgiving. However, in the Old Testament, the indispensability of God's justice, in accordance with the infinite laws of the universe, was made manifest, which appeared severe and vengeful. Within the New Testament, the merciful character of God was revealed in Christ's atonement, which unveiled compassion and forgiveness. The phenomenon of the simultaneous congruency of God's justice and mercy is represented in the example of a debtor who foolishly racked up an overwhelmingly enormous bill, one he would never be able to repay. It would not be just or fair to the merchant, that such a vast debt be waived. Justice demanded the sum either be repaid and the debtor becoming a slave to the merchant, as he pursued endless labor to repay some portion of his obligation, or else the debtor be imprisoned by law, suffering his lost life of freedom, as he endeavored to pay to society the consequence of his foolish crime. Justice seemed harsh but this was what he deserved.

Fortunately for the debtor, along came a wondrous Benefactor, who agreed to pay the merchant the unimaginable sum owed, satisfying the demands of justice. The Benefactor now "owned" the debtor and was entitled to set the terms of repayment but instead, the Benefactor granted him a life of freedom. The only condition was, henceforth, he must follow his Law, which would be a devoted life of faithfulness, a cleansing of past mistakes, continual repentance as needed, and an attempt to emulate his purity and goodness, in the spirit of his wondrous Benefactor. Acceptance of such a condition allowed for the generous Benefactor to bestow mercy upon the fool, to satisfy the demands of justice for his careless sin, and to demonstrate his profound love for him. Through his grace, He provided complete forgiveness as his miraculous gift.

Jesus Christ, The Savior of the World, is the Spiritual Benefactor of all mankind. As an Unblemished and Perfect being, He was the only one capable of satisfying the demands of justice and extending the arm of mercy and grace to the foolish and flawed inhabitants of this fallen world. But for those workers of evil, who are unwilling to accept their Spiritual Benefactor's miraculous gift, they must pay justice themselves. Terrifying biblical phrases, such as, fires of hell (Deuteronomy 32:22), outer darkness, weeping, wailing, gnashing of teeth (Matt. 8:12), are horrific images of the inescapable demands of justice. Still, God continually pleads that all come to him, for He has already paid justice, suffering beneath the deepest abyss of pain and sorrow, for anyone willing to accept his magnanimous gift of mercy and grace. Then in the final judgement, when God declares Justice has been served, all will receive their due rewards: Each beautiful and glorious in its own measured degree, as is a heaven of stars, or moon, or sun.[30]

* * *

Christ's atonement not only paid justice for sins, but it covered human frailties and weaknesses, pains and suffering, inadequacies, and limitations. "For I can do everything through Christ, who gives me strength" Philippians 4:13 (NLT). Human beings can accomplish great things through practice and development of their physical, intellectual, and emotional faculties, but when they invite God into their lives and allow His Omnipotence to enhance their efforts, those accomplishments are magnified beyond anything imagined.

It is the same in cases of healing and recovery. God is anxious for those suffering to call on him so He might provide aid in lightening their loads. ". . . (He) himself took on our infirmities and bare our sicknesses" Matt. 8:17 (KJV). It is his almighty power that amplifies anything they might do on their own. He suffered all things, as He Atoned for the sins, pains, and weaknesses of everyone. "Jesus said, 'Come to me, all you who are weary and carry heavy burdens, and I will give you rest. Take my yoke upon you. Let me teach you, because I am humble and gentle at heart, and you will find rest for your souls'" Matt. 11:28-29 (NLT). "'For my yoke is easy, and my burden is light'" Matt. 11:30 (KJV). When two oxen are yoked together (with a device like a harness), they equally share the load that they pull. When an individual is yoked, or harnessed, with God, the load is not equal; He carries more of it because He is the all-powerful God, therefore, the burden the individual carries feels light.

To take advantage of the Lord's atonement, one must accept those conditions set by him. His Law is faith, repentance, baptism, and reception of the Holy Spirit. As each utilizes faith and demonstrates sincere efforts towards repentance, consistently showing small signs of improvement in the aspiration to that perfection, which is God's, he/she draws upon his miraculous power. Therefore, through a series of beginner steps and actions, individuals combine patience in the recovery process, with an awareness of continuing the necessary exertion towards healing, while the Lord comforts, lifts the burdens, and eases their pains, often healing them completely, spiritually and physically (God willing.)[31] It requires time and effort for heart, mind, and body to recuperate, and it is a singular blessing to have friends, family, religious, wellness, or other support and recovery groups eager and anxious to help throughout the healing stages. If anyone is willing to begin or continue the habit of scripture reading and attending worship services, this always contributes to the healing process. The reading and hearing of God's own words, and those recorded by the prophets in the Bible, individually, or among families and friends, allows inspiration to open and divine interaction occurs through God's Holy Spirit. He reveals, motivates, and encourages with spiritual influences that are unique to individual circumstances or family concerns. The Spirit reminds us He answers prayers by providing peace, comfort, and recognition that one's burdens are being eased, even if not completely removed. He usually "speaks" to his children in a calm, quiet voice, bestowing a soothing balm in any stage of illness or injury, even if complete healing has not yet occurred.

Innermost prayers that express hope, love, and gratitude, privately or in worship services, are always a means of speaking to God, and intimations received through reverent prayer, study, and meetings are his way of "speaking" back. His words are not heard by ear, but they are experienced by sensing heartfelt warmth or tears of joy and by perceiving impressions that come to mind during the still and serene moments. Of course, God does not answer on command; He always allows each of His children to work through difficulties and grow by faith. With increased consistency and attempts to make small steps toward behavioral and habitual progress, one becomes more aware of a greater presence in his/her life. It is one that comforts, inspires, guides, loves, and empowers.

Losing a loved one is certainly one of the most difficult challenges in life because the painful loss and separation feels so permanent. Sometimes it seems healing isn't even possible. Many people innately believe there will be a joyful and heavenly reunion with their loved one. Others are inconsolable in their loss, wondering if they will ever see them again. But the knowledge and firm assurance of such a reality distills through the power of His Holy Spirit.

Through consistent efforts in prayer, study, and worship, one can refine the senses that recognize those reassuring impressions God places in the mind, and the warmth/joy he imparts to the heart. So, while the loved one is still missed and longed for daily, the comfort and peace, received from the affirmation of an eventual reunion, does provide healing to a once hopeless and grieving soul.

* * *

It did for me, and it took a long time, but this is the essence of faith, isn't it?

We continually struggle to hope and believe it is not only a possibility, but a reality. Sometimes, it seems as though the faith-prayer-study-worship formula is one that works for others but, for some reason, we imagine it will not work for us. Why is that? A formula, or a recipe, always works when the steps are followed exactly. Isn't it the same as constructing a machine or a building, increasing physical muscle, losing weight, conquering powerful addictions, or any other process? If we follow instructions, they work. The problem is we give up, we quit, we get frustrated, discouraged, or think it is taking too long so it must not be possible—and just when we are almost "there." But we waste so much time and energy fighting the process only to come short of success. If we only would open our hearts and minds to allow God's visionary spark of hope to inspire and motivate us to soldier toward the ultimate assurance of the noble goal, then we would reach success. That goal for me included the desired healing, happiness, comfort, peace, and perspective of the prized reward: eventual reunion with my long-lost loved one.

* * *

True repentance includes genuine remorse for sins committed, a course correction and redirection onto a path of improvement, and restitution (whenever possible) to those injured by sinful actions. As with healing, repentance requires time and effort because the heart, mind, and habits need to change. But through God's atonement, as the sincere person works through the process, the weight of sin lifts and He guarantees complete forgiveness. ". . . though your sins are like scarlet, I will make them as white as snow; though they are red like crimson, I will make them as white as wool" Isaiah 1:18 (NLT).

Jesus was baptized by John the Baptist in the River Jordan to set the example, as He demonstrated the necessity to fulfil all righteousness. "Jesus answered, Verily, verily, I say unto thee, except a man be born of water and of the Spirit, he cannot enter into the kingdom of God" John 3:5 (KJV). Baptism is one of the requirements of His law, which represents a cleansing of past sins and is symbolic of burying the old self in water, then coming forth out of the water as a renewed self, born again of the Spirit, in holiness, service and commitment to God.

And service to God, which is accomplished by serving loved ones and fellowmen, is one of the most effective means of inviting inspiration and communion with His Holy Spirit. Providing service allows individuals to demonstrate concern, and to develop love for others. It builds personal confidence and self-worth as they experience the love God has for everyone, and it brings true gratitude and peace into the lives of both those who serve and those who are the recipients of the service.

The Lord enjoys the efforts his children make towards travel in this new path forward as they determine to progress towards a better way of life. Everyone's journey will be different from another's. No one competes with anyone else but only with him or herself. To use a marathon metaphor, each runs his/her own race, and is, hopefully, continuing to improve upon his/her own time. Small changes that take place gradually are not usually evident from one day, week, or month to the next. But if one takes a momentary step back to look with a hindsight view over many months or years, surprisingly, there are many enlightening manifestations of incremental gains which have occurred from miniature, consistent efforts. And in the race of life, regardless of the obstacles encountered along the course, God *can* heal broken hearts and minds, give hope in times of despair, provide aid through daily difficulties, and eventually reunite families forever, as He provides assured salvation, and offers eternal life with God, though His grace. [32]

In the same way as the wondrous Benefactor did not owe the debtor anything but volunteered to aid him in his hopeless predicament, God owes mankind nothing. However, He willingly volunteered to aid each foolish and fallen individual because of the unconditional love He has for everyone. Not only did He provide immortality for them, He promised an eternal inheritance of everything He has, to anyone willing to covenant with Him, in the same way Sarah and Abraham did. The Apostle Paul told the disciples once all are baptized unto Christ (His Gospel), there are no divisions among them, but they are the children of God and heirs to the promises made to Abraham: "And all who have been united with Christ in baptism have put on Christ, like putting on new clothes. There is no longer Jew or Gentile, slave or free, male and female. For you are all one in Christ Jesus. And now that you belong to Christ, you are the true children of Abraham. You are his heirs, and God's promise to Abraham belongs to you" (Gal. 3:27-29/NLT).

♫ HEAL YOUR BROKEN HEART

Say there - did you lose your way? Out there - so far from home
Say there - just take my hand, you're going to need me
This road's way too long

Aftermath! These are the trying times
And when you're low, don't know where to go
Don't know how to start, Morning sun shines off the glowing grace
And there's a welcome place, it's time to heal your heart

Say there - don't lose your faith or where I am you can't come
Dangers - they're all about, just fix your sight on my eyes
and you've won

Aftermath! These are the trying times
And when you're low, overcome with woe, don't give up -
just start
Morning sun shines off the glowing grace, and there's a
welcome place
It's time to heal your broken heart

Anger's rage is intense and there's no hope if you give way, I
give you comfort
My peace I leave with you, don't trouble your heart, be not
afraid

So there - I'll wipe your tears, I've got your loved ones just
waiting here
Seek me - I'm just as real as your dreams, Try me
Come soar on the power of my wings

Morning sun shines off the glowing grace, and there's a welcome place ♪
It's time to heal your broken heart

* * *

The doctrine of The Church of Jesus Christ of Latter-day Saints states Christ saves by grace, and each one does the best he/she can do in mortality. This is confirmed by the passages, in James: "Even so faith, if it hath not works, is dead, being alone" James 2:17 (KJV). "Now someone may argue, 'Some people have faith; others have good deeds.' But I say, 'How can you show me your faith if you don't have good deeds? I will show you my faith by my good deeds. You say that you have faith, for you believe that there is one God. Good for you! Even the demons believe this, and they tremble in terror. How foolish! Can't you see that faith without good deeds is useless?'" James 2:18-20 (NLT). "Was not Abraham, our father, justified by works when he offered Isaac, his son, on the altar?" James 2:21 (KJV). "You see, his faith and his actions worked together. His actions made his faith complete. And so, it happened just as the Scriptures say: 'Abraham believed God, and God counted him as righteous because of his faith.' He was even called the friend of God. So, you see, we are shown to be right with God by what we do, not by faith alone" James 2:22-24 (NLT). "Likewise, also, was not Rahab, the harlot, justified by works when she had received the messengers and had sent them out another way? For as the body without the spirit is dead, so faith without works is dead also" James 2:25-26 (KJV).

When the children of Israel were preparing to enter the Promised Land, they sent spies to Jericho to assess the situation they would encounter upon their entrance into the city. When they arrived at Rahab's (the prostitute) house, she allowed the spies to lodge there. The king of Jericho learned of the spies and told Rahab to turn them over to him. But she said they had already left her home, while, in fact, she hid them on her roof by covering them with flax stalks. She told the spies that the rumors in town of the Israelites' escape from the Egyptians, through the dried-up Red Sea, had preceded them and the town was astonished and afraid of them. "And as soon as we heard these things, our hearts did melt, neither did there remain any more courage in any man, because of you . . ." Joshua 2:11 (KJV). She believed the Hebrew God was the Lord of heaven and earth, and she wanted to learn more of him and his ways when the children of Israel returned to inhabit the land. The spies left a blessing on her household, swore an oath they would remember to deal kindly and truthfully with her family upon their return, then escaped back to the prophet Joshua. They reported to him how, truly, the Lord had delivered the city into their hands because the entire town was in awe of the Israelite God and nation.[33]

Latter-day Saint Christians believe in trying their best to live the Gospel of Jesus Christ, patterning their lives after His teachings, serving their families, neighborhoods, churches, communities, nations, and fellowmen worldwide. Nevertheless, all are sinners and fall short of perfection. But they demonstrate through their good works how they desire to obey God, they have faith in him, and they believe His atonement and grace are the means whereby they are saved.

Another way to understand the role efforts play in the attempt to do one's best is explained in a devotional by Brad Wilcox, professor of ancient scripture at BYU, in which he explains grace vs. works using the story of a mom providing music lessons for her child: "Mom pays the piano teacher. Because Mom pays the debt in full, she can turn to her child and ask for something. What is it? Practice! Does the child's practice pay the piano teacher? No. Does the child's practice repay Mom for paying the piano teacher? No. Practicing is how the child shows appreciation for Mom's incredible gift. It is how he takes advantage of the amazing opportunity Mom is giving him to live his life at a higher level. Mom's joy is found not in getting repaid but in seeing her gift used—seeing her child improve. And so, she continues to call for practice, practice, practice. If the child sees Mom's requirement of practice as being too overbearing ("Gosh, Mom, why do I need to practice? None of the other kids have to practice! I'm going to be a professional baseball player, anyway!"), perhaps it is because he doesn't yet see with Mom's eyes. He doesn't see how much better his life could be if he would choose to live on a higher plane."

"In the same way, because Jesus has paid justice, He can now turn to us and say: 'Follow me,' (Matthew 4:19) 'Keep my commandments' (John 14:15). If we see His requirements as being way too much to ask, maybe it is because we do not yet see through Christ's eyes. We do not yet comprehend the improvement He is trying to make in us."[34]

FOLLOW ME ♪

Where do words begin to sing songs of honor my heart brings
Tokens worthy to convey thankfulness enough to pay
Wretch I am – I pray escape, so mold, conform me to thy shape
If you love me, follow me, and love me: Feed my sheep

Then I say to you, my friend, draw near and I'll be there
Heed my voice, abide my truth, my light dispels all fear

And now my strength embolden grows, "Impossible," I do
    not know
A sense, your presence leads the way, unveil thy face, I'm beg-
    ging you to stay
When life's curtain shall unfold, reveal assurance, sanctify
    me whole
If you love my, follow me, and love me: Feed my sheep

When the choruses shall ring, praise and glories soar on wing
Wondrous plan, eternal love, thy golden skies proclaim above:
Well done, thou good and faithful one, you followed me & now
    the day is done
Thy joy is full, come enter in and love me: Lead my sheep ♫
If you love me, follow me, and love me: Feed my sheep

54

8

THE GATHERING

1 Kings 12 records the reign of Rehoboam, son of Solomon, at the time when a division occurred between the twelve tribes of Israel, mainly because of a long rivalry between Judah and Ephraim. The tribe of Judah primarily occupied the south, and the tribes of the other ten separated to the north.[35] (The tribe of Levi received an inheritance of Priesthood, as it ministered among all the tribes, particularly, overseeing the responsibilities of the tabernacle). ". . . When all Israel realized that the king refused to listen to them, they responded, 'Down with the dynasty of David! We have no interest in the son of Jesse. Back to your homes, O Israel! Look out for your own house, O David!'" 1Kings 12:16 (NLT) "So (Northern) Israel rebelled against the house of David unto this day" 1Kings 12:19 (KJV).

Later, under the reign of Hoshea, the ten tribes of Israel rebelled against the Lord.[36] In about 721 B.C.,[37] Assyria swept out of the north, captured the Northern Kingdom of Israel, and carried the tribes away into captivity.[38] After many wars and conquests, the ten tribes became lost and scattered throughout all nations. They now no longer know they are chosen descendants of Abraham, Isaac, and Jacob (Israel).

The southern kingdom of Judah was conquered and scattered by Babylon around 587 B.C. Roughly seventy years later, some returned to their land, where they remained a nation until the Romans scattered them again throughout all the world (about 135 A.D).[39]

When Jacob was dying, he gave blessings to his twelve sons, Rueben, Simeon, Levi, Judah, Zebulun, Issachar, Dan, Gad, Asher, Naphtali, Joseph, and Benjamin. He particularly blessed Joseph (through Joseph's two sons, Ephraim, primarily, and Manasseh) to be the most numerous of the tribes. ". . . Jacob crossed his arms as he reached out to lay his hands on the boys' heads. He put his right hand on the head of Ephraim, though he was the younger boy, and his left hand on the head of Manasseh, though he was the firstborn . . . But Joseph was upset when he saw that his father placed his right hand on Ephraim's head . . . 'No, my father, this one (Manasseh) is the firstborn' . . . 'I know it, my son; I know,' he replied. 'Manasseh will also become a great people, but truly his younger brother will become even greater. And his descendants will become a multitude of nations'" Gen. 48:14, 17-19 (NLT). Israel continued his son, Joseph's, blessing saying, ". . . The blessings of thy father have prevailed above the blessings of my progenitors unto the utmost bound of the everlasting hills: They shall be on the head of Joseph . . . on the crown of the head of him that was separate from his brethren'" Gen. 49:26 (KJV).

Jacob also gave a special blessing to his son, Judah, declaring his authority and leadership position among the family and the world, until the Messiah comes: "Judah, your brothers will praise you. You

will grasp your enemies by the neck. All your relatives will bow before you" Gen. 49:8 (NLT). "The scepter shall not depart from Judah, nor a lawgiver from between his feet, until Shiloh come, and unto him shall the gathering of the people be" Genesis 49:10 (KJV).

Today the term, *Israel*, is primarily associated with the Jewish state because the tribe of Judah was never lost, only scattered. The Jewish people have always maintained their identity, history, culture, traditions, and religion. Although all the tribes were scattered throughout the world for their disobedience and rebellion, God has used their scattering to bless the world. There is symbolism in the children of Israel's recorded wilderness wanderings, disobedience, and trials, as it figuratively represents the wanderings, disobedience, and trials of all people, since each one struggles through his/her own dark clouds, braving stormy seasons, in search of the anticipated shining tomorrows.

Additionally, the people of Judah carried with them in their wanderings the Law and the recorded wisdom and vision of the prophets, which included the commandments, the genealogy of their fathers, God's interaction with man, and his message of hope, gratitude, love, life, and peace. They were chosen to light the world with this message throughout the ages. The Old Testament also contained prophesies concerning the coming of the Messiah and foretold how He would descend from the line of David but would be rejected (except for a following of disciples). He would bring everlasting light and salvation when He would make his soul an offering for sin and make intercession for the transgressors.

"And there shall come forth a rod out of the stem of Jesse, and a Branch shall grow out of his roots: and the spirit of the Lord shall rest upon him, the spirit of wisdom and understanding, the spirit of counsel and might, the spirit of knowledge and of the fear of the Lord . . . and he shall not judge after the sight of his eyes, neither reprove after the hearing of his ears: But with righteousness shall he judge the poor, and reprove with equity for the meek of the earth..." Isaiah 11:1-4 (KJV).

"For he shall grow up before him as a tender plant, and as a root out of dry ground; he hath no form nor comeliness; and when we shall see him, there is no beauty in him that we should desire him. He is despised and rejected of men; a man of sorrows and acquainted with grief, and we hid, as it were, our faces from him; he was despised, and we esteemed him not. Surely, he hath borne our griefs and carried our sorrows . . . He was wounded for our transgressions and was bruised for our iniquities: the chastisement of our peace was upon him; and with his stripes we are healed" Isa. 53:2-5 (KJV).

"All we like sheep have gone astray; we have turned everyone to his own way; and the Lord hath laid on him the iniquity of us all.

He was oppressed, and he was afflicted, yet he opened not his mouth; he is brought as a lamb to the slaughter, and as a sheep before her shearers is dumb, so he openeth not his mouth . . . And he made his grave with the wicked and with the rich in his death; because he had done no violence, neither was any deceit in his mouth . . . Yet it pleased the Lord to bruise him... when thou shalt make his soul an offering for sin . . . the pleasure of the Lord shall prosper in his hand. Therefore, will I divide him a portion with the great and he shall divide the spoil with the strong; because he hath poured out his soul

unto death; and he was numbered with the transgressors; and he bare the sins . . . and made intercession for the transgressors" Isa. 53:6-7, 9-10, 12 (KJV).

Isaiah's prophesies of the Son of God were among the greatest, and he foresaw the time when Christ would gather all the children of Israel. "And it shall come to pass . . . that the Lord shall set his hand again the second time to recover the remnant of his people, which shall be left from Assyria, and from Egypt . . . and from the islands of the sea. And he shall set up an ensign for the nations, and shall assemble the outcasts of Israel, and gather together the dispersed of Judah from the four corners of the earth. The envy also of Ephraim shall depart, and the adversaries of Judah shall be cut off: Ephraim shall not envy Judah, and Judah shall not vex Ephraim. But they shall fly upon the shoulders of the Philistines toward the west . . . they shall lay their hand upon Edom and Moab; and the children of Ammon shall obey them . . . And there shall be an highway for the remnant of his people, which shall be left from Assyria; like as it was to Israel in the day that he came up out of the land of Egypt" Isa. 11:11-14, 16 (KJV).

Isaiah's vision of the symbolic highway foresaw the comforting of Zion as the gathering of the House of Israel would occur before Christ's second coming. The Jewish people have a returned homeland in Israel, and the Lord is remembering the covenant he made with all the House of Israel. As distant but familiar truths ring true to the lost tribes, God is leading them back to *Abraham's Covenant*, the everlasting covenant He made with Sarah and Abraham: "Hearken to me, ye that follow after righteousness, ye that seek the Lord . . . Look unto Abraham your father and unto Sarah that bare you: for I called him alone, and blessed him, and increased him" Isa. 51:1-2 (KJV). "For the Lord will comfort Israel again and have pity on her ruins. Her desert will blossom like Eden, her barren wilderness like the garden of the Lord. Joy and gladness will be found there. Songs of thanksgiving will fill the air" Isa. 51:3 (NLT).

"Hearken unto me, my people; and give ear unto me, O my nation . . . My righteousness is near; my salvation is gone forth, and mine arms shall judge the people; the Isles shall wait upon me, and on mine arm shall they trust" Isa. 51: 4-5 (KJV).

"Those who have been ransomed by the LORD will return. They will enter Jerusalem singing, crowned with everlasting joy. Sorrow and mourning will disappear, and they will be filled with joy and gladness. . . I am the Lord your God, who stirs up the sea, causing its waves to roar. My name is the LORD of Heaven's Armies. And I have put my words in your mouth and hidden you safely in my hand . . . I am the one who says to Israel, 'You are my people'" Isa. 51: 11, 15-16 (NLT).

Jesus, himself, declared he would recover the house of Israel: "And then will I gather them in from the four quarters of the earth; and then will I fulfill the covenant which the Father hath made unto all the people of the house of Israel. . . . If the Gentiles will repent and return to me . . . behold, they shall be numbered among my people, O House of Israel. And blessed are the Gentiles because of their belief in me, in and of the Holy Ghost, which witnesses unto them of me and of the Father . . . Then will I remember my covenant which I have made unto my people, O house of Israel . . ." 3 Nephi 16:5,6,11,13.[40]

At the end of Christ's life, He pronounced on the cross, "It is finished; Father, into thy hands I commend my spirit." Indeed, his earthly mission was complete. He came to Earth to fulfil the

Law of Moses, to teach by example, to establish His Church, to perform mighty miracles that all may gain a glimpse of His power and goodness, and, most importantly, to provide the atonement and resurrection so that, in fact, all mankind would be saved to live again.

"Behold, I am Jesus Christ, whom the prophets testified shall come into the world" 3 Nephi 11:10. ". . . I am Jesus Christ, the Son of God. I created the heavens and the earth and all things that in them are. I was with the Father from the beginning. I am in the Father, and the Father in me; and in me hath the Father glorified his name . . . and the scriptures concerning my coming are fulfilled. And as many as have received me, to them have I given to become the sons of God; and even so will I to as many as shall believe on my name, for behold, by me redemption cometh and in me is the law of Moses fulfilled" 3 Nephi 9:15-17.

"I am the light and the life of the world. I am Alpha and Omega, the beginning and the end. Behold I have come into the world to bring redemption unto the world, to save the world from sin. Therefore, whoso repenteth and cometh unto me as a little child,  him will I receive, for of such is the kingdom of God. Behold, for such I have laid down my life, and have taken it up again; therefore repent, and come unto me ye ends of the earth..." 3 Nephi 9: 18, 21-22.

LET YOUR LIGHT SO SHINE ♫

Let your light so shine that all may see your good works
And glorify your Father, who is in Heaven, holy
You must light the world, don't hide beneath a bushel
I am with you forever, your faith hath made you whole

9

THE WARNING

The First Presidency of the Church of Jesus Christ of Latter-day Saints declared in a statement in 1995, *The Family: A Proclamation to the World*, ". . . that marriage is between a man and a woman . . ."[41] The late Apostle, L. Tom Perry, stated in 2015,, ". . . the solid majority of mankind still believes that marriage should be between one man and one woman. We need to remind ourselves . . . of the wonderfully reassuring and comforting fact that marriage and family are still the aspiration and ideal of most people and that we are not alone in those beliefs."[42]

Throughout the world's history, when desperate times called for desperate measures, exceptions were made. Death, disease, war, famine, and other disasters which threatened the extinction of God's people triggered his command to declare such an exception. However, as is evidenced by the model story of Sarah and Abraham, exceptions to the rule have not come without consequences: Heartbreak and suffering has always been the inevitable result of interference into the lives of devoted couples and their families and has had destructive after-effects through the generations that followed. Although the tragedy in the Middle East is the extreme example, historically, to one degree or another, deviation from the rule has indubitably caused unavoidable agony and turmoil.

The Church of Jesus Christ of Latter-day Saints states in *The Family: A Proclamation to the World*, "The family is ordained of God.

Marriage between man and woman is essential to His eternal plan. Children are entitled to birth within the bonds of matrimony, and to be reared by a father and a mother who honor marital vows with complete fidelity… Further, we warn that the disintegration of the family will bring upon individuals, communities, and nations the calamities foretold by ancient and modern prophets."

In the Book of Revelation (KJV), God provided John a vision of events, detailed in the book with seven seals. The seals are understood to represent thousand-year periods in the earth's existence, and the sixth and seventh seals reveal the earth's commotion, disasters, fires, destruction, and desolation, prior to the second coming of the Savior, Jesus Christ.[43] The Book of Mormon, a companion to the Bible that also chronicles God's dealings with his people, details His promises to those who walk with him in sincerity of heart.

Although these times can be troublesome, despairing, chaotic, and fearful, God promises peace, not as we know it by the world's definition, but as He explains it in Scripture: "I am leaving you with a gift—peace of mind and heart. And the peace I give is a gift the world cannot give, so do not be troubled or afraid," John 14:27 (NLT.)

My affinity to counterparts of other faiths comes from the emotional attachment I have to my Swedish-Lutheran relatives and roots. The honest souls of all denominations and persuasions who seek truth are dear to me. I felt comfort when I learned of God's love for his children and His well-conceived, all-inclusive plan. It truly is ingenious and miraculous! He knows everyone's heart, and He judges individuals based on their sincere attempts to do the best with the knowledge they have. In as much as they strive to live according to their consciences, He blesses them and promises rewards that strengthen and enlighten. And he taught us in John 13:34 (KJV,) "A new commandment I give unto you, that ye love one another, as I have loved you." These soothing words provide me with the hope we may find unity and determination, even in these times of division and confusion.

* * *

The only glimpse ever provided of a celestial state is the Garden of Eden, in which the Lord created Adam and Eve and placed them. The Garden was a heavenly paradise of unparalleled beauty and abundance, immune to death, mortal pain, and suffering. "Then the Lord God planted a garden in Eden in the east, and there He placed the man he had made. The Lord God made all sorts of trees grow up from the ground—trees that were beautiful and that produced delicious fruit. In the middle of the garden he placed the tree of life and the tree of knowledge of good and evil . . ." Gen. 2:8-9 (NLT). "And the Lord God caused a deep sleep to fall upon Adam . . . and He took one of his ribs . . . And the rib, which the Lord had taken from man, made He a woman . . . And Adam said, 'This is now bone of my bones and flesh of my flesh . . ." Gen. 2:21-23 (KJV). "This explains why a man leaves his father and his mother and is joined to his wife, and the two are united into one" Gen. 2:24 (NLT).

"And the Lord God warned him (Adam), 'You may freely eat the fruit of every tree in the garden, except the tree of the knowledge of good and evil. If you eat its fruit, you are sure to die . . .'" Genesis 2:16-17 (NLT). "Now the serpent was the shrewdest of all the wild animals the Lord God had made. One day he asked the woman, 'Did God really say you must not eat the fruit from any of the trees in the garden?' 'Of course, we may eat fruit from the trees in the garden,' the woman replied. 'It's only the fruit from the tree in the middle of the garden that we are not allowed to eat. God said: You must not eat it or even touch it; if you do you will die.' 'You won't die!' the serpent replied to the woman. 'God knows that your eyes will be opened, as soon as you eat it, and you will be like God, knowing both good and evil . . .' The woman was convinced. She saw how the tree was beautiful, and its fruit looked delicious, and she wanted the wisdom it would give her. So, she took some of the fruit and ate it. Then she gave some to her husband . . . and he ate it too. At that moment, their eyes were opened, and they suddenly felt shame at their nakedness. So, they sewed fig leaves together to cover themselves" Gen. 3:1-7 (NLT).

"Then the Lord God said, 'Look, the humans have become like us, knowing both good and evil. What if they reach out, take fruit from the tree of life, and eat it? Then they will live forever!' So, the Lord God banished them from the Garden of Eden, and he sent Adam out to cultivate the ground from which he had made them.

After sending them out, the Lord God stationed mighty cherubim to the east of the Garden of Eden. And he placed a flaming sword . . . to guard the way to the tree of life" Gen. 3: 22-24 (NLT).

So, it was that Adam and Eve fell from innocence and purity, after they had partaken of the tree of knowledge of good and evil. Cheribum were placed to guard their access to the tree of life so they would not partake of the fruit of the tree and live forever in their fallen state. They had suffered (a spiritual) death, as they were warned, and eventually, they would suffer temporal death, as a result of their fall. They were driven out of Eden's paradise and made to travel the journey of mortality, walk by faith, covenant with God, learn from mistakes, develop charity, and achieve personal growth in the recognition of good and evil. At the end of their journey, they would leave behind this life, taking with them only the knowledge they had gained from their earthly experience, and the relationships they had formed. Eventually, through the resurrection and atonement of Jesus Christ, they would gain salvation and eternal life, reunite with their family, and return to the presence of God, partaking *forever* of the Tree of Life.

"And now, my sons, I speak unto you for your profit and your learning; for there is a God and He hath created all things, both the heavens and the earth, and all things that in them are, both things to act and things to be acted upon. And to bring about his eternal purposes in the end of man . . . after he had created our first parents, it must needs be that there was an opposition; even the forbidden fruit in opposition to the tree of life; the one being sweet and the other bitter. Wherefore, the Lord God gave unto man that he should act for himself. Wherefore, man could not act for himself save it should be that he was enticed by the one or the other . . . Wherefore, he said unto Eve, yea, even that old serpent, who is the devil, who is the father of all lies, wherefore he said: 'Partake of the forbidden fruit and ye shall not die, but ye shall be as God, knowing good and evil'. And after Adam and Eve had partaken of the forbidden fruit, they were driven out of the Garden of Eden, to till the earth. And they have brought for children, yea, even the family of all the earth" 2 Nephi 2:14-16,18-2.

"And the days of the children of men were prolonged, according to the will of God, that they might repent while in the flesh; wherefore, their state became a state of probation and their time was lengthened, according to the commandments which the Lord God gave unto the children of men. For he gave commandment that all men must repent; for he showed unto all men that they were lost because of the transgression of their first parents . . ." 2 Nephi 2:21.

"And now, behold, if Adam had not transgressed, he would not have fallen, but he would have remained in the Garden of Eden. And all things which were created must have remained in the same state in which they were created; and they must have remained forever and had no end. And they would have had no children, wherefore they would have remained in a state of innocence, having no joy, for they knew no misery; doing no good, for they knew no sin. But behold, all things have been done in the wisdom of Him that knoweth all things" 2 Nephi 2:22-24.

"Adam fell that men might be, and men are that they might have joy. And the Messiah cometh in the fullness of time that He may redeem the children of men from the fall" 2 Nephi 2:25-26.

♫ TWO BY TWO

Two by two there was an ark that filled
With couples feathered, furry, scaled and billed
As well as those pairs of the human kind
The key words double, twosome, binary and duo seem to
    come to mind

Adam/Eve, Old Abe and Sarah, Mary/Joseph, Liz/Zacharias
Jimmy/Gloria, John and Janie, see – and you and me
So, when you're feeling sad and lonely
Just recall each other's one-and-only is
Somewhere out there for eternity

Cats and dogs, together, shoes and socks
Peas and pods, suede/leather, time and clocks
Ham and eggs, salt/pepper, curds and whey
The magic number's two, Want to fix a world that's blue
It's clear as night and day

Adam/Eve, Old Abe and Sarah, Mary/Joseph, Liz/Zacharias
Gayle/Pete, and John and Janie, see – and you and me
So, when you're feeling sad and lonely
Just recall your one-and-only is
Somewhere, ever after, and yours exclusively

Your better half comes complete with her own tainted wings
Or your bright prince requires some days his neck to wring
But he's your best friend and she's your damsel to defend
It's a fight to the finish to never diminish a trust that just
    will never end!

(Sometimes) Life deals a blow, Cross o'er that snow
Into a land, That's glorious and grand
Though there's a break, soon o'er that lake, there'll come the day
When true love replays

Adam/Eve, Old Abe and Sarah, Mary/Joseph, Liz/Zacharias ♪
Jimmy/Roselyn, John and Janie, see – there's even you and me
So, when you're feeling sad and lonely, just recall your
    one-and-only is
Somewhere - oh, they're out there - for eternity

10

THE TRIUMPH

WHERE IS LOVE ♫

Long ago, surrounded by a vision far away
There was peace upon the land and rays of sun warmed every day
But now clouds of darkness loom to stifle any star ♪
Seizing hopes within a cage and trapping light within a heart

Where is love, where did it go, where is love, the east winds blow
Where is love, when will it show, if there were love, I would follow

There's a boy who questions what the future dares to bring
And a girl who wants to help their dreams live more than anything
In a world of trouble and a time of loneliness
Heartbreak threatens any sign of triumph over fear unless

There is love (but), where did it go, where is love, the east
    winds blow
Where is love, when will it show, if there were love, I would follow

In the open air, birds will sing their song
Spring is everywhere, it coaxes buds along
Life begins anew, what else can it do ♪
You must press the winds to swell, it all depends on you ♪

Where is love, where did it go, where is love, the east winds blow
Where is love, when will it show, if there were love, I would follow

There is an enormous amount of commotion in today's world. While much of the technological activity is invaluable, so much of its noise is distracting and disturbing. It is important to schedule time each day to center on meaningful prayer and scriptural meditations, otherwise, they will be forced out by the demands of busy routines. And they are immeasurably important because they provide small reprieves from life's overwhelming troubles and concerns. Slowing down to make time for matters of true significance may be one of the greatest challenges of the times. Prioritizing family and developing a relationship with God is surely life's most prized accomplishment. Bible teachings are classic ones; they apply to every generation because all experience the human condition. When reading his Word, a perspective opens that enables bible students to see their surroundings and others through God's eyes. Lessons learned often create a less divisive and antagonistic atmosphere, as well as, more kind, loving, just, and compassionate individuals, families, congregations, and communities. Even among the difficulties of life, God will soothe sorrowful and disappointing situations by illuminating His peaceful, supportive, and joyful influences through His Holy Spirit.

* * *

I often reflect on my early picturesque youth. We are all born so innocent and humble. We long to learn, love, be loved, and hope with childlike wonder for a happy future. I can only imagine, in the same way earthly parents prepare their children for the best in life they can, were there not meticulous preliminaries that accompanied our send-offs from a heavenly home? We must have been so joyous and eager to embark on a grand mortal adventure. Did exuberant festivities celebrate the forthcoming mind/body/spirit opportunities? Would we have ever agreed to such risk and suffering if we had not already glimpsed the unbelievable, priceless payoff? And how could we ever find our way back to the place where we belong?

Part of those meticulous preliminaries certainly must have included the heavenly gift of an inner compass, tracking device, and honing capabilities that would ensure that guiding sense *homeward*. The abundance of worldwide religious and spiritual propensities validates the acknowledgement and yearning most have for transparency of some vague, but deep-seated, *before* experience. We all share the driving impulse to connect with the profound and meaningful. But the noise and distraction of physical surroundings nearly guarantees an interference from the central radar, our holy guide. As if by design, there seems to be a built-in mechanism through which we are drawn inward to our core navigation system. It is the suffering, pain, challenge, adversity, desperation, and longing that assures our ascendant cries of distress will ultimately invoke that miraculous Godly intervention, which delivers us from hopelessness and darkness into recovery and light.

I have prayed a lifetime for the miracle of my brother's healing. But, as it apparently turns out, this was not the miracle in store, at least not in this world. I am grateful, though, for incredible siblings who all enjoy, support, and love the occasions we spend with him. Instead, my quest for life's meaning and God's love has led me to an unequivocal knowledge of and personal relationship with Jesus Christ, the Creator of the Universe—how unbelievable and spectacular does that even sound? And, the miracle of it all is, not only how the Almighty is aware and intimately involved in individuals' lives, but the reality of such spiritual intimacy yields an enthusiastic determination to encourage others to seek This Redeemer of Mankind, The Savior of the World, thereby guaranteeing them the same transformational hope, happiness, and healing, as I have astonishingly and awesomely appreciated being able to encounter.

* * *

It was the best of times; it was the worst of times. Indeed, we see the best and the worst of these times all around us. The best of times is evident in the miracle of the Savior's atonement, which affects and improves the lives of good people everywhere. Conversely, the worst of times is continually displayed in the horrific chosen evil acts of men and women, which spread fear, divisiveness, and destruction, and pervade the 24-hour news cycle. However, there is hope and optimism for the future. The Scriptures declare that if we are prepared, there is no need to fear.[44]

Preparation includes the study of The Law and The Prophets, and the understanding of the importance of covenants. Specifically, realizing the significance of Abraham's Covenant opens hearts and minds to unimaginable possibilities and extraordinary capabilities! It instills confidence in the Resurrection and in God's plan of happiness for his children. Even though life is replete with sorrow and loss, there is comfort and healing in the knowledge of a lasting reunion with loved ones.

In fact, heaven truly does heal the heart by revealing that the love experienced in life does not end with physical death. There is hope in understanding how the family is key in God's eternal plan for happiness. It is the unit of heaven and it is the element that makes us all members of the family of God, the children of God: And if all are children of God, then all are heirs of God, through the atonement of Jesus Christ, by way of Abraham's Covenant. The entire religious Judeo-Christian world understands the prominent nature of the family and its intricate role in the realization of personal fulfillment and joy, and in societal stability and cohesion. They recognize, through the book of Genesis, Sarah and Abraham are the covenant couple and Isaac is their heir to the blessings promised them. And it has become evident, through Sarah and Abraham's standard; the same eternal blessings apply to all who are willing to walk with God in their efforts to draw closer to Him.

We have much in common with our fellow friends of faith. We also have a tremendous opportunity, as well as a sobering responsibility, to study and understand the scriptures through the power of the Holy Spirit. We extend the invitation to our

faithful friends to share with us in these scriptures, which provide insight, comfort, healing, and peace in a time of darkness, chaos, decline, and fear.[45] Likewise, we ask our friends to share with us their rich histories and traditions of hope and faith, whatever that faith may be.

All faiths have origins in God and offer spiritual perspectives which help us come to a more complete understanding of our own religions. Some religious examples include the ancient wisdom of the Far East proverbs, the intent of the Hebrew Bible, or the accomplishments of our fellow Christians, including the heroic biblical scholars of the past and of the present. A common sense of contribution and commitment invests everyone in that noble purpose, which unites and strengthens, enabling the protection of freedom, family, and a religious way of life. God created mankind in his image, and He loves all his children. He can inspire any sincere and humble individual with a portion of his word. Everyone has one point to gain, another to offer; and there is wisdom to be learned from religions of the world, where there is generally a belief in God, love and respect of family, concern for humanity, and fervent reverence for the majesty of his creations.

Today's modern tale of good versus evil must include a cheerful army of dedicated "do-gooders" to ensure a story that ends with the triumph of light and truth over darkness and deceit.[46] When all is said and done, heaven's healing message of the Bible, whether in the beginning or in the end, is that ". . . God is love,"[47] and truly, "Love conquers all . . ."[48]

♫ BATTLE HYMN OF THE REPUBLIC
(3rd Verse)

In the beauty of the lilies Christ was born across the sea
With a glory in His bosom that transfigures you and me
As He died to make men holy, let us live[49] to make men free
While God is marching on.

Glory, glory, hallelujah, Glory, glory, hallelujah
Glory, glory, hallelujah, His truth is marching on[50] ♫

DISCUSSION POINTS

CHAPTER 1: THE BIBLE

1. Discuss your own thoughts on the best elements of these times and the worst ones.

2. What do you love about the Bible?

3. Has the Bible influenced your life? If so, in what way? If not, are you considering exploring it?

4. Do you recall a certain sermon or biblical story that impressed you? What thoughts and feelings do you recall? Did it inspire you with questions or motivations? What would you like to do with those?

5. Review Sarah and Abraham's story and discuss their relationship in the Bible. Can you identify any similarities that your story may have with theirs?

6. What are key takeaways you have learned from them?

CHAPTER 2: THE THREAT

1. What are some of the current threats to society and the Bible you have perceived in today's political climate and popular culture?

2. Why do you think God and the Bible are under attack and in what ways do you see the results of those attacks?

3. What are your thoughts on why oppressive regimes attempt to limit parents' influence over their children? Can you identify examples of this in modern society?

4. Give some reasons that these same regimes find it necessary to eliminate religion, the Bible, and cohesive, functioning families.

5. Discuss your thoughts on the rewriting of history, its agenda and the consequences; what benefit is there to studying the good and bad aspects and events in history?

6. Do you want to save the Bible and our American society? If so, how would you go about doing so?

Song *Balloons*: What thoughts come to your mind when you read or listen to *Balloons*? What concerns do you sense?

CHAPTER 3: THE COVENANT

1. Do you have a love story? Discuss Sarah and Abraham's love story and their covenant with God.

2. Discuss the blessings God promised them through this covenant.

3. What did God intend in guaranteeing Ishmael (Hagar's son) a great nation? Name a way in which you see a manifestation of his greatness.

4. Analyze the significance of Abraham's trial to sacrifice Isaac, his only child of the covenant; what can we learn from Abraham's faith?

5. Explain the difference between a covenant and a birthright. Can you think of a covenant you have ever made with someone or with God? How do you think you are honoring that covenant? What would you like to improve?

6. Why did God covenant with Sarah and Abraham and why does He covenant with all His people?

Song *A Better Friend:* How does beginning to understand God's covenant with Sarah and Abraham invite a new chapter of hope into your life?

CHAPTER 4: THE COUPLE

1. Would you like to have a love story of your own? How does Sarah and Abraham's covenant affect you?

2. What do we learn in, Matthew 22, as Jesus exchanged with the Sadducees?

3. God covenanted with Abraham that He would bless him, conditional upon what terms? (Discuss Abraham's responsibility.)

4. Study the effect of free will on an individual or couple's heavenly reward.

5. Explore your thoughts regarding true love. Might you consider any changes to improve your chances of finding love or of improving your relationship?

6. What steps can you take to make your marriage last? Having a clear goal in mind, as a couple, will enhance your relationship. Suggest some things that would help you accomplish your goal(s).

7. What thoughts do you have on the benefits of considerate, honest communication in your marriage/relationship? What roles do service and friendship play in a successful marriage?

8. Consider how strengthening your relationship with God might contribute to enhancing your marriage and family relations?

Song *On Your Side*: If you are ½ of a couple, examine some of the dreams you have for the two of you. If you aren't, examine your dreams for a permanent future relationship. What actions are you taking? What additional actions might you consider?

CHAPTER 5: THE PLAN

1. Examine God's plan. Who does this plan include?

2. What thoughts come to your mind regarding Jesus' second coming. Discuss your thoughts and desires.

3. Analyze the Apostle, Paul's statement, "Now, if there is no resurrection, what will those do who are baptized for the dead? If the dead are not raised at all, why are people baptized for them?" What do you think he means?

4. Analyze your thoughts regarding the significance of the Ten Commandments and of the Law of Moses.

5. Contemplate the significance of the atonement of Jesus Christ. What does his higher spiritual law require of you?

Song *Oh, Remember*: Are you able to recognize God's goodness throughout your day? How does it make you feel when you remember it? Why do you think the scriptures speak often of *remembering*?

CHAPTER 6: THE DREAMS

1. Consider Joseph's relationship with his ½ brothers; contemplate and discuss his family dynamic and his relationship with God.

2. Describe Joseph's attitude and experiences in Egypt; what were some things he was able to accomplish with his gift?

3. Compare Joseph's betrayal and sale into slavery to the Savior's betrayal and sale unto death.

4. Reflect on your personal thoughts of Jesus Christ's atonement and resurrection. Any comments you are willing to share on paper or with others?

5. Is this the first exposure to the concept of Christ's atonement? What thoughts do you have? What questions come to mind?

6. Are you able to recognize any gifts God has given you? If so, what have you been able to do in your life with some of those gifts?

If not, write down 5 things for which you are grateful that have happened this week. Does this inspire you in any way to use any of your gifts or blessings to fulfill your dreams?

Song *Non-Stop to O'Hare:* How have your difficulties lead you to new attitudes and outcomes?

CHAPTER 7: THE BENEFACTOR

1. Are you in need of healing? List three pains or injuries from which you desire relief.

2. List some of the rewards (gifts) you would like to receive from God. Discuss the relationship your faith has to your efforts. Evaluate two things you might do this week to enhance your relationship with God (Church attendance, daily prayer, begin Bible study, less TV/more thought-provoking meditation, more family time, etc.)

3. Specifically, in what ways has Bible study, in combination with church attendance, improved your life? If you have recently begun your Bible study and church attendance, journal your thoughts, impressions, and feelings you are experiencing. Review them weekly to observe any patterns emerging or improvements you begin to see and note them on paper.

4. Identify several steps you might take to improve your relationships. Now list several strategies to begin implementing them. (Choose one night per week to schedule 1-3 hours with your family, spouse, parent, etc., combine some Bible study/prayer with [a] loved one[s], more consistent Church attendance and/or participation activities, etc.)

5. Can you think back to a time when someone helped you out? Write a paragraph, detailing how it made you feel; explore some of your thoughts, emotions, and events you might have encountered at the time.

6. Consider a family member, friend, co-worker, neighbor, fellow-parishioner, stranger, or other whom you might help in some way this week. Make a three-step plan to implement your strategy of service (1. Analysis or prayers to determine someone to help; 2. What to do (cut their grass, babysit, drop off a snack or meal, pay a visit, etc.; 3. Journal your thoughts on your experience, how did the experience make you feel, reflect on possible follow-ups, etc.)

7. Choose a flaw or shortcoming upon which you would like to improve. What steps can you begin towards your repentance? Develop a 3-step plan to initiate the process of change. Keep a daily journal of your successes and drawbacks this week. Notice if you observe any good patterns or any perceived problems. Consider a small prize or bonus with which to reward yourself for your weekly efforts.

Song *Heal Your Broken Heart:* Consider some of the thoughts or images you have when you listen to or read this song. Does the song inspire you with optimism for healing? Identify one optimistic impression you received.

Song *Follow Me:* Can you list a couple of changes you might make to become a better follower of God?

CHAPTER 8: THE GATHERING

1. List three lessons that might be learned from the scattering of Israel.

2. Analyze some of the reasons the Israelites were chosen to be God's people. Explain some leadership responsibilities given to the tribe of Judah? Evaluate Jacob's blessings given to his son, Joseph. Why do you think Joseph had special blessings?

3. Discuss your thoughts regarding the coming of "Shiloh," as mentioned in Genesis 29:10.

4. Describe several of Isaiah's prophesies concerning Jesus Christ, the Son of God.

5. It has been stated that the birth of Jesus was the most significant event in the history of all the world. Contemplate this statement and evaluate some of the reasons for its validity.

6. Can you feel God's love for you? In what ways do you feel it? Imagine a short list of things you might do to feel His love more completely in your life. Write it down, revisit it, & make adjustments accordingly.

Song *Let Your Light So Shine*: Why do you think it is important to be a light to those around you? What relationship do you see to light and faith, faith and light? (Matt. 5:14-16, Mark 5:25-34)

CHAPTER 9: THE WARNING

1. Explore the significance of Adam and Eve's creation, their experience in the Garden of Eden, and the purpose of their downfall.

2. Explain the reason God placed Cherubim and a flaming sword to guard the Tree of Life? In what way do Adam and Eve's experiences relate to you?

3. Think about biblical/prophetic warnings that have been given. Discuss the purpose of warnings (are they to scare us, to prepare us, to enlighten us, to guide us, to bless us, etc.)? Identify warnings that are applicable for society today. What types of things can you do once you have been warned?

4. Life is full of obstacles and difficulties. List and explain ways, specifically, that you can find joy amid your troubles. Discuss the statement: Gratitude is an attitude.

5. Do you see any relationship between Adam and Eve and Sarah and Abraham? What significance do Adam and Eve have in enabling your mortal journey? What significance do Sarah and Abraham have in enabling your spiritual journey?

6. What messages of importance have you learned from the Bible? Create a list and adjust or add to it accordingly.

Song *Two by Two*: What other magic numbers of "two" come to mind? (apples/oranges, black and blue, etc.) Have some fun with your thoughts on the significance of pairing in language.

CHAPTER 10: THE TRIUMPH

1. List and explain 5 elements that indicate the best of times and the worst of times to you. Write two index or flash cards to remind yourself to make time to enjoy a couple of favorite activities. Place one card on the bathroom mirror and one on the refrigerator. Note several pleasant ways you can prepare yourself to triumph in your life.

2. Describe 3 details you have learned about Abraham's covenant with God. How does your understanding of these lessons help with healing in your life? Write or discuss your answers.

3. Reflect on some of the possible benefits of multi-religious interactions. List 3 friends of another faith and several things your beliefs have in common. How might you strengthen your friendships? How might these friendships strengthen your faith? How might faith and friendships strengthen your community?

4. Itemize five ways in which you are feeling and seeing God's love in your life. What are ways you can return forgiveness or kindness to someone whom you think has offended you. Write a paragraph explaining your thoughts on the phrases, "God is Love" and "Love Conquers All." In what ways do you think God's love could help you conquer the ills in your life and/or in today's society? Can you think of 1 thing you might want to do to experiment with His love to improve or "fix" something?

5. Please outline a short strategy (5-7 steps) for achieving your personal and spiritual potential now that you have a deeper appreciation of God's concern for you and your loved ones? List those steps, indicating actions for the facilitation of your

victorious outcomes. (1. Find a good/better job, complete GED, bachelor's/master's degree, vocational training, etc.; 2. Daily exercise; 3. Write a book, poem, or song; 4. Greater participation in social improvements, etc.) As you observe developing changes, remember to share your smile with others you contact!

Song *Where Is Love*: Review your ideas on the significance of God's love in your healing process. Imagine yourself one year from now: Write down some images you see and emotions you look forward to feeling? Identify pleasantries you have encountered in the process. Review your notes. Acknowledge and celebrate your achievements monthly! Congratulations on your many successes, you, beautiful shining STAR in the universe, you!

ACKNOWLEDGEMENTS

Many thanks to the extremely talented artists I have encountered along my path. A special thanks to Ryan Hale for the sophisticated technical and creative contributions to the music, which continue to inspire me.

Thank you to Drs. Joel Strom and Ron Sloan for the years of productive and adventuresome opportunities. Trenée Brown, you are a source of encouragement; Lynn Woodbury, you inspire my indomitable spirit; and to John, Nan, and Rick for the laughs, tears, and endless reinforcement! Todd Johnson: Thank you, for the singular photos, and Mark and Shelly, for your expert photography!

I want to express a special appreciation to Chaplain Samuel McGinn, on behalf of Reverend Franklin Graham, for your time and consideration, leading to the inspirational and delightful exchange. Many thanks to Kary, Nanette, and an entire team of supportive experts!

Finally, and most of all, a very special thank you, Mom and Dad, for the example of love, devotion, and service you showed to one another, to each of us, and to all those your exemplary lives touched. I love you always, and forever: Until we meet again…

END NOTES

[1] Charles Dickens, *A Tale of Two Cities*, 1859

[2] (Complete reference: Genesis 12:10-20)

[3] Genesis 15-16

[4] Producer Lee Groberg, for BYU TV, "*Fires of Faith: The Coming Forth of the King James Bible*," https://www.byutv.org/Show/123d4a82-3d47-488e-beda-2496a5a1ff2c

[5] Trent Toone, *BYU Tells the Story of the King James Bible in the 'Fires of Faith*, Deseret News; Published Saturday, Oct. 15, 2011

[6] Holy Bible, New Living Translation, Introduction to the New Living Translation, p. A15. Tyndale House Publishers, Inc., Carol Stream, Illinois

[7] Toone 2011, op. cit.

[8] The Bible Study Site, http://www.biblestudy.org/basicart/bible-errors.html

[9] Wikipedia, Lenin

[10] Notable Quotes, http://www.notable-quotes.com

[11] Nikita Khrushchev, *Speech to Western Diplomats* at Polish Embassy, Moscow, 18 Nov. 1956

[12] Ezra Taft Benson (1899-1994); President of the Church of Jesus Christ of Latter-day Saints; served two terms as President Eisenhower's Secretary of Agriculture: Said in a 1966 Brigham Young University address that Khrushchev made the statement during a one-on-one discussion the two had in September 1959

[13] Tom Kershaw, 2012, https://hollowverse.com/Joseph_Stalin

[14] Joshua Goode, Professor of History & Cultural Studies, Claremont Graduate University; The History Channel https://www.history.com/topics/russia/joseph-stalin-video

[15] Wikipedia, Joseph Stalin

[16] Kershaw 2012, op. cit.

[17] Ibid.

[18] Christopher Tatara, 2013, *"Hitler, Himler, and Christianity in the Early Third Reich,"* Illinois Wesleyan University, ctatara@iwu.edu

[19] Ibid

[20] Ibid.

[21] *The Doctrine & Covenants* 84:35-38 (vs. 38)

[22] Bradley, Jared, jareds@prageru.com, Prager U, http://www.prageru.com; Anthony Rivera, Church of Jesus Christ of Latter-day Saints, Public Affairs, Menifee, CA Stake arivera.harvard@outlook.com

[23] *The Pearl of Great Price*; The Book of Abraham

[24] *The Doctrine & Covenants 84:35-38*

[25] *The Pearl of Great Price*; The Book of Abraham

[26] *Bible Dictionary*, Sadducees (KJV)

[27] Pearl of Great Price, Moses 1:39

[28] Doctrine & Covenants 138:47-48, The Prophet Elijah was to plant in the hearts of the children the promises made to their fathers; foreshadowing the great work to be done in the temples of the Lord... for the redemption of the dead, and the sealing of the children to their parents, lest the whole earth be smitten with a curse and utterly wasted at his coming.

[29] Old Testament, Genesis, chapters 41-46

[30] Sons of perdition (presumably counted on one hand and who remain unidentified in Scripture) are the infinitesimal exception (John 17:12, Thessalonians 2:4, Doctrine & Covenants 76:43).

[31] New Testament, Matthew 6:10, "Thy kingdom come. Thy will be done in earth, as it is in heaven."

[32] *The Book of Mormon*, Mosiah 3:17, "And moreover, I say unto you, that there shall be no other name given nor any other way nor means whereby salvation can come unto the children of men, only in and through the name of Christ, the Lord Omnipotent."

[33] Old Testament, Joshua 2

34 Bradley Ray Wilcox, 2011, *"His Grace Is Sufficient,* https://speeches.byu.edu, Professor of Ancient Scripture at Brigham Young University.

35 Mark Lee, mlee@manatt.com, Gospel Doctrine Teacher, Westwood I, CA, The Church of Jesus Christ of Latter-day Saints

36 Old Testament, 2 Kings 17:7-18

37 Bible dictionary, Assyria

38 Old Testament, 2 Kings 17:5-6

39 Brief History of the Scattering of Israel, "appendix-scatter," *Book of Mormon Student Manual* (2009), 415

40 *Book of Mormon*

41 "*A Proclamation to the World*," By the First Presidency and Council of the Twelve Apostles of The Church of Jesus Christ of Latter-day Saints, Read by Gordon B. Hinckley as part of his message to the General Relief Society Meeting held September 23, 1995, Salt Lake City, Utah

42 April 2015, General Conference of the Church of Jesus Christ of Latter-day Saints, "*Why Marriage and Family Matter – Everywhere in the World,*" L. Tom Perry, Quorum of the Twelve Apostles

43 Revelation 5:1, John describes seeing a book in the right hand of God, locked with seven seals (which seals are understood to represent periods of time throughout the Earth.)

44 *Doctrine & Covenants 38:30*, "…if ye are prepared ye shall not fear."

45 Scriptures available at https://ChurchofJesusChrist.org

46 New Testament, John 16:33, "…be of good cheer, I have overcome the world."

47 New Testament, 1 John 4:8, "He that loveth not, knoweth not God; for God is love."

48 Virgil (Publius Vergilius Maro) Roman author/poet, born October 15, 70 B.C. "Love conquers all things; let us, too, surrender to Love"

49 The original version says *let us die to make men free*, referencing the Civil War era.

50 Julia Ward Howe (text), 1819-1910; Music: Anon., ca. 1861

ABOUT THE AUTHOR

Kristy Landgren is an author, musician, and faith-based coach who helps people find hope, happiness, and healing through word and song. She, herself, has become transformed, after struggling with faith and loss in her life. Now she uses the power of God's word to help others find the completeness they seek. She lives in Los Angeles and loves to travel to visit family and friends.

Connect at:

https://kristylandgren.com
https://www.openupyourheart.net
https://www.facebook.com/kristy.landgren
https://www.facebook.com/KristyLandgrenTheHeavenHealsSeries
https://twitter.com/ivorytunes
https://www.instagram.com/kristylandgren/
https://www.linkedin.com/in/kristin-kristy-landgren-a5257857/